WeightWatchers®

The fantastic flavours of Italy

Easy Italian

First published in Great Britain by Simon & Schuster UK Ltd, 2012
A CBS Company

Copyright © 2012, Weight Watchers International, Inc.
Simon & Schuster Illustrated Books, Simon & Schuster UK Ltd,
First Floor, 222 Gray's Inn Road, London WC1X 8HB

www.simonandschuster.co.uk

Simon & Schuster Australia, Sydney
Simon & Schuster India, New Delhi

Weight Watchers, **ProPoints** and the **ProPoints** icon are the registered
trademarks of Weight Watchers International Inc. and are used under
license by Weight Watchers (UK) Ltd.

Weight Watchers Publications: Cheryl Jackson, Jane Griffiths,
Selena Makepeace, Nina McKerlie and Imogen Prescott.

Recipes written by: Sue Ashworth, Sue Beveridge, Tamsin Burnett-Hall,
Cas Clarke, Siân Davies, Roz Denny, Nicola Graimes, Becky Johnson, Kim Morphew,
Joy Skipper, Penny Stephens and Wendy Veale as well as Weight Watchers Leaders
and Members.

Photography by: Iain Bagwell, Steve Baxter, Steve Lee, Juliet Piddington and
William Shaw.
Project editor: Nicki Lampon.
Design and typesetting: Geoff Fennell.

Colour reproduction by Dot Gradations Ltd, UK.
Printed and bound in China.

A CIP catalogue for this book is available from the British Library

ISBN 978-0-85720-934-4

1 2 3 4 5 6 7 8 9 10

Pictured on the title page: Creamy chicken pasta p82.
Pictured on the introduction: Italian rice salad p28, Gourmet pizza p46, Lasagne p58.

WeightWatchers®

The fantastic flavours of Italy

Easy Italian

SIMON &
SCHUSTER
ILLUSTRATED

London · New York · Sydney · Toronto · New Delhi

A CBS COMPANY

Weight Watchers **ProPoints** Weight Loss System is a simple way to lose weight. As part of the Weight Watchers **ProPoints** plan you'll enjoy eating delicious, healthy, filling foods that help to keep you feeling satisfied for longer and in control of your portions.

🟡 This symbol denotes a vegetarian recipe and assumes that, where relevant, free range eggs, vegetarian cheese, vegetarian virtually fat free fromage frais, vegetarian low fat crème fraîche and vegetarian low fat yogurts are used. Virtually fat free fromage frais, low fat crème fraîche and low fat yogurts may contain traces of gelatine so they are not always vegetarian. Please check the labels.

❄ This symbol denotes a dish that can be frozen. Unless otherwise stated, you can freeze the finished dish for up to 3 months. Defrost thoroughly and reheat until the dish is piping hot throughout.

Recipe notes

Egg size: Medium sized, unless otherwise stated.

Raw eggs: Only the freshest eggs should be used. Pregnant women, the elderly and children should avoid recipes with eggs that are not fully cooked or raw.

All fruits and vegetables: Medium sized, unless otherwise stated.

Stock: Stock cubes are used in recipes, unless otherwise stated. These should be prepared according to packet instructions.

Recipe timings: These are approximate and meant to be guidelines. Please note that the preparation time includes all the steps up to and following the main cooking time(s).

Microwaves: Timings and temperatures are for a standard 800 W microwave. If necessary, adjust your own microwave.

Low fat spread: Where a recipe states to use a low fat spread, a light spread with a fat content of no less than 38% should be used.

Low fat soft cheese: Where low fat soft cheese is specified in a recipe, this refers to soft cheese with a fat content of less than 5%.

Contents

Introduction

Packed full of fantastic food from the best of Weight Watchers cookbooks, *Easy Italian* will bring the taste of Italy right into your home. Conjuring up visions of hot sunny days and leisurely meals with family and friends, this book just sings of the Mediterranean.

From antipasti (starters) to dolci (desserts), there is plenty here to choose from. For a light meal, try delicious soups such as Italian Bean and Rosemary Soup, fantastic bruschettas or a classic Tomato and Basil Platter. Family favourites include delicious pizzas and pastas such as Mushroom, Spinach and Ham Calzone, Orecchiette with Pork Ragù or Pasta Puttanesca. For a stunning supper, try dishes such as Mediterranean Roasted Steak, Italian Haddock Bake or Aubergine Parmigiana. Whatever you try, all these recipes are easy to prepare and full of flavour and Italian flair.

About Weight Watchers

For more than 40 years Weight Watchers has been helping people around the world to lose weight using a long term sustainable approach. Weight Watchers successful weight loss system is based on four tried and trusted principles:

- Eating healthily
- Being more active
- Adjusting behaviour to help weight loss
- Getting support in weekly meetings

Our unique **ProPoints** system empowers you to manage your food plan and make wise recipe choices for a healthier, happier you. To find out more about Weight Watchers and the **ProPoints** values for these recipes contact Customer Services on 0845 345 1500.

Storing and freezing

There are many recipes in this book that can be frozen. Once you have mastered the art of cooking delicious healthy meals, you may want to make extra and store or freeze it for a later date. Store any leftovers in sealed containers in the fridge and use them up within a day or two. Many recipes can be frozen, as can individual ingredients, but it is important to make sure you know how to freeze safely.

- Wrap any food to be frozen in rigid containers or strong freezer bags. This is important to stop foods contaminating each other or getting freezer burn.
- Label the containers or bags with the contents and date – your freezer should have a star marking that tells you how long you can keep different types of frozen food.
- Never freeze warm food – always let it cool completely first.
- Never freeze food that has already been frozen and defrosted.
- Freeze food in portions, then you can take out as little or as much as you need each time.
- Defrost what you need in the fridge, making sure you put anything that might have juices, such as meat, on a covered plate or in a container.
- Fresh food, such as raw meat or fish, should be wrapped and frozen as soon as possible.
- Most fruit and vegetables can be frozen by open freezing. Lay them out on a tray, freeze until solid and then pack them into bags.

- Some vegetables, such as peas, broccoli and broad beans can be blanched first by cooking for 2 minutes in boiling water. Drain, refresh under cold water and then freeze once cold.
- Fresh herbs are great frozen – either seal leaves in bags or, for soft herbs such as basil and parsley, chop finely and add to ice cube trays with water. These are great for dropping into casseroles or soups straight from the freezer.

Some things cannot be frozen. Whole eggs do not freeze well, but yolks and whites can be frozen separately. Vegetables with a high water content, such as salad leaves, celery and cucumber, will not freeze. Fried foods will be soggy if frozen, and sauces such as mayonnaise will separate when thawed and should not be frozen.

Shopping hints and tips

Always buy the best ingredients you can afford. If you are going to cook healthy meals, it is worth investing in some quality ingredients that will really add flavour to your dishes. When buying meat, choose lean cuts of meat or lean mince, and if you are buying prepacked cooked sliced meat, buy it fresh from the deli counter. Packaged cooked meat usually has salt and preservatives added.

We've added a checklist here for some of the store cupboard ingredients used in this book. Just add fresh ingredients in your regular shop and you'll be ready to cook the delicious recipes in *Easy Italian*.

Store cupboard checklist

- [ ] artichokes, canned in water
- [ ] artificial sweetener
- [ ] baking powder
- [ ] butter beans, canned
- [ ] cannellini beans, canned
- [ ] capers
- [ ] chilli (flakes and powder)
- [ ] chocolate (minimum 70% cocoa solids)
- [ ] cocoa powder
- [ ] cooking spray, calorie controlled
- [ ] coriander, ground
- [ ] cornflour
- [ ] couscous, dried
- [ ] crab meat, canned
- [ ] cumin, ground
- [ ] fennel seeds
- [ ] flour (plain and self raising)
- [ ] fruit, canned in natural juice
- [ ] garam masala
- [ ] gelatine
- [ ] herbs, dried (mixed and Italian)
- [ ] honey, runny
- [ ] horseradish sauce
- [ ] lasagne sheets, dried no precook
- [ ] lentils, dried
- [ ] mayonnaise, extra light
- [ ] mushrooms, dried porcini
- [ ] nutmeg
- [ ] oil (vegetable and olive)
- [ ] olives in brine (black and green)
- [ ] passata
- [ ] pasta, dried
- [ ] paprika
- [ ] pearl barley, dried
- [ ] peppercorns
- [ ] peppers, piquante
- [ ] pizza mix
- [ ] polenta, dried
- [ ] rice, dried (white and brown)
- [ ] saffron
- [ ] salt
- [ ] stock cubes
- [ ] sugar, caster
- [ ] tomato purée
- [ ] tomatoes (canned and sun-dried in oil)
- [ ] tuna, canned in brine
- [ ] vanilla essence
- [ ] vinegar, balsamic
- [ ] Worcestershire sauce
- [ ] yeast, fast action

Lunches and light bites

Mediterranean seafood soup

Serves 6

162 calories per serving

Takes 20 minutes to prepare,
30 minutes to cook

1 red pepper, de-seeded and
quartered

1 yellow pepper, de-seeded
and quartered

1 tablespoon olive oil

1 large onion, sliced thinly

½ fennel bulb, sliced thinly

100 ml (3½ fl oz) white wine

3 garlic cloves, sliced finely

grated zest and juice of a
small orange

a pinch of saffron threads

850 ml (1½ pints) fish stock

230 g can chopped tomatoes

200 g (7 oz) baby new
potatoes, quartered

250 g (9 oz) skinless white
fish fillet (e.g. coley),
chopped roughly

250 g (9 oz) mixed seafood,
defrosted if frozen

freshly ground black pepper

1 tablespoon chopped fresh
parsley, to garnish

If you're looking for a comforting meal, this hearty soup is packed with flavour. It's a complete meal in a bowl.

1 Preheat the grill to high and place the peppers on the grill rack, skin side up. Grill for 6–8 minutes, until the skin is blistered. Transfer to a bowl, cover and cool for 10 minutes or so and then peel off the skin and roughly chop the peppers.

2 Meanwhile, heat the olive oil in a large, lidded, non stick saucepan. Stir in the onion and fennel and cook gently for 10 minutes until softened, but not coloured.

3 Increase the heat, pour in the wine and stir in the garlic. Cook for about 2 minutes or until the wine has evaporated.

4 Add the orange zest and juice, saffron, fish stock, tomatoes and new potatoes. Season with black pepper to taste and bring to a simmer. Cover and cook for 20 minutes.

5 Stir the peppers and any juices that have collected in the bowl into the pan, along with the chopped fish. Replace the lid and gently poach for 3 minutes.

6 Finally, stir in the mixed seafood and heat through for 2 minutes. Serve ladled into warmed bowls and scatter the parsley on top.

Variation... For a Mediterranean vegetable soup, use vegetable stock instead of fish stock, omit the fish fillet and mixed seafood, and add two diced courgettes along with the grilled peppers.

Roasted tomato and red pepper soup with garlic croûtes

Serves 4

137 calories per serving

Takes 10 minutes to prepare,
45 minutes to cook

Ⓥ

❄ (soup only)

6 tomatoes, skinned (see Tip)
and halved

3 red peppers, de-seeded and
cut into quarters

calorie controlled cooking
spray

4 x 2.5 cm (1 inch) slices
French stick or 8 slices
French baguettine

1 garlic clove, halved

450 ml (16 fl oz) vegetable
stock

salt and freshly ground black
pepper

A summery soup with all the flavour of the Mediterranean.

1 Preheat the oven to Gas Mark 6/200°C/fan oven 180°C.

2 Place the tomatoes and peppers on a baking tray and spray
with the cooking spray. Roast for 40 minutes.

3 Remove the tomatoes and peppers from the oven and blend
using a food processor or hand held blender.

4 Spray a clean baking tray with the cooking spray and place
the slices of French bread on it. Rub the bread with the garlic
clove, spray with the cooking spray and cook in the oven for
3–5 minutes, until starting to brown and crisp.

5 Meanwhile, mix together the blended vegetables and stock
and warm through in a saucepan. Season.

6 To serve, top each bowl of soup with a croûte or croûtes.

**Tip... To skin the tomatoes, place them in a small bowl,
cover with boiling water for 30–60 seconds and then peel.**

Italian bean and rosemary soup

Serves 6

76 calories per serving

Takes 15 minutes to prepare +
overnight soaking, 1¼ hours
to cook

Ⓥ

❄

250 g (9 oz) dried cannellini
beans

calorie controlled cooking
spray

2 garlic cloves, crushed

1 large onion, diced

1 large carrot, peeled and
diced

8 fresh rosemary sprigs,
leaves chopped finely

2 litres (3½ pints) vegetable
stock

salt and freshly ground black
pepper

*A little planning is needed for this recipe if you are using
dried beans as they need to be soaked overnight. For a
quick canned bean alternative, see the Tip below.*

1 Place the cannellini beans in a bowl, cover with water and
leave to soak overnight.

2 Heat a large non stick saucepan and spray with the cooking
spray. Add the garlic, onion and carrot and gently fry for about
4 minutes until beginning to soften, adding a splash of water
if they start to stick.

3 Drain the beans, rinse well and drain again. Add the beans,
rosemary and stock to the pan and bring to the boil. Boil for
10 minutes, skimming the top occasionally, then keep at a low
simmer for 40–50 minutes or until the beans are tender.

4 Carefully remove half the soup to a blender and whizz until
smooth. Return to the pan and stir it in. Check the seasoning
and then serve.

Tip... Use canned beans for a much faster recipe. Add
3 x 300 g cans of cannellini beans, rinsed and drained,
to the sautéed vegetables. Reduce the stock to 1.2 litres
(2 pints) and reduce the cooking time to 10 minutes.

Variation... Use any small beans such as flageolet, pinto,
black eyed or haricot blanc.

Chunky vegetable and salami soup

Serves 4

194 calories per serving

Takes 10 minutes to prepare, 25 minutes to cook

❅

calorie controlled cooking spray

1 onion, diced

2 carrots, peeled and diced

2 celery sticks, diced

1 garlic clove, crushed

60 g (2 oz) dried small pasta shapes

400 g can chopped tomatoes

600 ml (20 fl oz) hot vegetable stock

110 g (4 oz) spinach, washed

75 g (2¾ oz) salami, cut into thin strips

salt and freshly ground black pepper

a handful of basil leaves, to garnish

Similar to a minestrone, this soup is almost like a stew. It's packed with vegetables and pasta and garnished with tasty strips of salami.

1 Spray a large, lidded, non stick saucepan with the cooking spray and heat until hot. Add the onion, carrots and celery. Stir fry for 5 minutes, adding a splash of water if the mixture starts to stick. Stir in the garlic and cook for a minute.

2 Add the pasta, tomatoes and stock. Bring to the boil, cover and simmer for 15 minutes until all the vegetables and pasta are tender. Remove from the heat and stir in the spinach. Season to taste. Cover and leave to let the spinach wilt.

3 Meanwhile, heat a small non stick frying pan until hot. Add the strips of salami and cook over a high heat for 1–2 minutes until crispy. Drain on kitchen towel.

4 Serve the soup in large bowls. Sprinkle over the salami and garnish with the basil leaves.

Variation... Cavolo nero is a fabulous green winter vegetable and a great alternative to spinach. Chop and add in step 2 for the final 5 minutes of cooking time.

Pesto chicken salad

Serves 4
199 calories per serving
Takes 10 minutes

**200 g (7 oz) sugar snap peas,
halved across**

2 tablespoons pesto sauce

**150 g (5½ oz) 0% fat Greek
yogurt**

**2 tablespoons extra light
mayonnaise**

**300 g (10½ oz) cooked
skinless boneless chicken
breasts, diced**

**1 red pepper, de-seeded and
cut into short strips**

150 g (5½ oz) crispy leaf salad

**salt and freshly ground black
pepper**

*Mixing pesto with yogurt and mayonnaise produces a light
sauce that works perfectly as a salad dressing.*

1 Bring a saucepan of water to the boil, add the sugar snap
peas and cook for 2 minutes until tender but still with some
bite. Drain and rinse in cold water.

2 In a bowl, mix the pesto sauce together with the yogurt and
mayonnaise, adding seasoning to taste.

3 Stir in the diced chicken, pepper and sugar snap peas. Serve
on a bed of crispy leaf salad.

Lamb bruschetta

Serves 2
238 calories per serving
Takes 15 minutes

calorie controlled cooking
  spray
**125 g (4½ oz) lean lamb leg
  steak, cut into thin strips**
1 onion, sliced
**75 g (2¾ oz) mushrooms,
  chopped**
**25 g (1 oz) sun-dried tomatoes
  in oil, drained**
**a fresh rosemary sprig, leaves
  only**
4 x 10 g (¼ oz) slices ciabatta
**1 garlic clove, peeled and left
  whole**

*Bruschetta is garlic rubbed toast and can be used as
a base for lots of dishes. Here it is topped with a great
combination of pan fried strips of tender lamb, mushrooms
and sun-dried tomatoes.*

1 Spray a non stick frying pan with the cooking spray and heat
until hot. Add the lamb, onion and mushrooms and stir fry for
3 minutes.

2 Add the sun-dried tomatoes and rosemary. Continue cooking
until the lamb is just brown. Add 2 tablespoons of water, reduce
the heat and simmer for 2 minutes.

3 Meanwhile, preheat the grill to medium and toast the
ciabatta on one side. Remove from the grill and immediately
rub the garlic clove vigorously over the toasted side of each
slice. Discard the garlic.

4 To serve, top each toast with the hot lamb mixture, dividing
equally.

⊙ **Variation...** For a tasty vegetarian version, see the recipe
on page 34.

Italian ham, fig and ricotta

Serves 1
177 calories per serving
Takes 2 minutes

2 fresh figs, halved
40 g (1½ oz) ricotta
**1 thin slice Parma ham, sliced
in half lengthways**

A super simple brunch for summery days.

1 Arrange the ingredients together on a plate, think of Italian summers and enjoy.

Turkey ciabatta grills

Serves 4
299 calories per serving
Takes 10 minutes

1 ciabatta loaf with sun-dried tomatoes or olives

2 tablespoons sun-dried tomato paste

150 g (5½ oz) grilled red and yellow pepper strips (see Tip)

8 x 25 g (1 oz) turkey rashers

salt and freshly ground black pepper

a few basil leaves, to garnish

Turkey rashers make a tasty topping for this quick lunch.

1 Preheat the grill to high.

2 Slice the loaf in half lengthways and spread with the tomato paste.

3 Top both pieces of ciabatta with the pepper strips and then the uncooked turkey rashers. Grill for 1½ minutes, turn the rashers over and grill for another 1½ minutes until the rashers are cooked.

4 Slice each piece of bread in half and serve, seasoned and scattered with a few basil leaves.

Tip... Look for grilled pepper strips in jars, preserved in vinegar, then rinse and drain them. Alternatively, you can buy canned red peppers (sometimes called pimientos), which simply need to be drained and sliced.

Variation... Buy plain ciabatta loaves if you can't find ciabatta with sun-dried tomatoes or olives.

King prawn, red onion and pepper bruschetta

Serves 2

347 calories per serving

Takes 10 minutes to prepare,
20–25 minutes to cook

1 red onion, cut into wedges

1 small red pepper, de-seeded
and sliced

1 small green pepper,
de-seeded and sliced

1 tablespoon olive oil

1 garlic clove, crushed

1 teaspoon balsamic vinegar

1 fresh thyme sprig

100 g (3½ oz) raw peeled king
prawns, defrosted if frozen

15 cm (6 inches) French stick,
halved horizontally

salt and freshly ground black
pepper

The perfect lunchtime snack with a bit of class.

1 Preheat the oven to Gas Mark 6/200°C/fan oven 180°C.
Line a roasting tin with non stick baking parchment.

2 Toss the red onion, peppers, olive oil, garlic and vinegar
together and place in the roasting tin with the thyme sprig.
Roast for 20–25 minutes until tender and beginning to char
at the edges, adding the prawns to the vegetables for the last
5 minutes of cooking time.

3 Toast the French bread on one side until golden. Top with
the roasted vegetables and prawns and season.

Tip... The vegetables can be roasted ahead of time. Perhaps
cook up a double batch, allow to cool and then keep in the
fridge for up to 3 days; they are equally delicious eaten
cold.

Variation... You could use the same amount of small prawns
if you prefer, but they won't look nearly as appetising as
the king prawns.

Italian rice salad

Serves 4
406 calories per serving
Takes 25 minutes

225 g (8 oz) dried long grain rice
2 tablespoons olive oil
2 tablespoons red wine vinegar
1 tablespoon lemon juice
a pinch of caster sugar
5 cm (2 inches) cucumber, chopped
12 baby plum or cherry tomatoes, halved
25 g (1 oz) pitted black olives, halved
100 g (3½ oz) mozzarella light, cut into chunks
4 beef tomatoes, thinly sliced
1 small red (or ordinary) onion, sliced into thin rings
salt and freshly ground black pepper

To serve
4 thin slices genuine Parma ham
about 12 basil leaves, torn into shreds

Full of flavour, this is ideal as a light lunch.

1 Bring a saucepan of water to the boil, add the rice and cook according to the packet instructions. Drain, rinse with cold water and drain again.

2 Make the salad dressing by whisking together the oil, vinegar, lemon juice and caster sugar. Season to taste.

3 Mix together the cucumber, plum or cherry tomatoes, olives, mozzarella and cold rice. Add the dressing and mix well.

4 Arrange the beef tomatoes and onion around the edge of four serving plates. Pile the rice salad in the middle and serve, garnishing each portion with a slice of Parma ham and basil leaves.

Tip... If you don't like olives, simply omit them from the recipe.

Tomato and basil platter

Serves 4

73 calories per serving

Takes 10 minutes to prepare
+ 30 minutes standing

Ⓥ

4 beef tomatoes, thinly sliced

**12 baby plum or cherry
tomatoes, halved**

**a bunch of spring onions,
finely chopped**

**a handful of basil leaves, torn
into shreds**

For the dressing

1 tablespoon olive oil

2 teaspoons lemon juice

1 garlic clove, chopped

**salt and freshly ground black
pepper**

Tomato and basil is a classic salad combination.

1 Arrange the beef tomatoes on a large serving platter, fanning out the slices. Top with the plum or cherry tomato halves and then sprinkle with the spring onions.

2 Mix together the olive oil, lemon juice and garlic. Season.

3 Sprinkle the dressing over the salad. Cover with cling film and leave at room temperature for about 30 minutes to allow time for the flavours to develop.

4 Scatter with the basil leaves and serve.

Tip... When all the different varieties of tomatoes are in season, it's a good idea to use them to make this fabulous salad.

Warm roasted prawn salad

Serves 4

204 calories per serving

Takes 15 minutes to prepare,
  35 minutes to cook

1 aubergine, cut into chunks

2 red onions, cut into wedges

300 g (10½ oz) butternut
  squash, peeled, de-seeded
  and cut into chunks

8 garlic cloves, peeled but left
  whole

1 lemon, cut into wedges

2 fresh rosemary sprigs

calorie controlled cooking
  spray

2 teaspoons fennel seeds

400 g (14 oz) raw king prawns,
  tail on, defrosted if frozen

60 g (2 oz) spinach, washed

60 g (2 oz) rocket

salt and freshly ground black
  pepper

2 tablespoons balsamic
  vinegar, to serve

Fish and seafood are an ideal choice for a meal.

1 Preheat the oven to Gas Mark 6/200°C/fan oven 180°C.
Place the aubergine, onions and squash in a large roasting tin
with the garlic, lemon and rosemary. Season, spray with the
cooking spray, scatter over the fennel seeds and roast for
25 minutes.

2 Remove from the oven, stir the vegetables and place the
prawns on top. Return to the oven for 10 minutes until the
prawns are cooked through and the vegetables lightly charred.
Remove and leave to cool slightly.

3 Divide the spinach and rocket between four serving plates
and top with the roasted vegetables and prawns. Drizzle over
the balsamic vinegar just before serving.

Tip... To use ready cooked prawns, spray a non stick frying
pan with cooking spray and fry over a medium heat for
1–2 minutes until hot, or add them cold to your salad.

Quorn bruschetta

Serves 2
162 calories per serving
Takes 15 minutes
Ⓥ

**calorie controlled cooking
    spray**
1 onion, sliced
**75 g (2¾ oz) mushrooms,
    chopped**
**25 g (1 oz) sun-dried
    tomatoes in oil, drained**
**a fresh rosemary sprig,
    leaves only**
**75 g (2¾ oz) Quorn Chicken
    Style Pieces**
**4 x 10 g (¼ oz) slices
    ciabatta**
**1 garlic clove, peeled and left
    whole**

*This is a fantastic vegetarian version of the recipe on
page 22.*

1 Spray a non stick frying pan with the cooking spray and
heat until hot. Add the onion and mushrooms and stir fry for
3 minutes.

2 Add the sun-dried tomatoes and rosemary. Cook for a couple
of minutes and then add the Quorn and 2 tablespoons of water.
Reduce the heat and simmer for 2 minutes.

3 Meanwhile, preheat the grill to medium and toast the
ciabatta on one side. Remove from the grill and immediately
rub the garlic clove vigorously over the toasted side of each
slice. Discard the garlic.

4 To serve, top each toast with the hot Quorn mixture, dividing
equally.

Sardines on pesto toasts

Serves 2
232 calories per serving
Takes 10 minutes

120 g can sardines in tomato
  sauce
2 medium slices wholemeal
  bread
1 tablespoon pesto sauce
1 tomato, sliced
a bunch of fresh basil,
  chopped roughly
freshly ground black pepper

A very quick and simple recipe using canned sardines in tomato sauce. Combined with a good wholemeal bread, pesto and fresh basil you have an aromatic light lunch.

1 Preheat the grill to hot. Place the sardines on a piece of foil on the grill pan and grill for 3–4 minutes.

2 Meanwhile, toast the bread, spread with the pesto sauce and arrange the tomato slices on top.

3 Spoon the warmed sardines and tomato sauce on top of the bread and scatter with the basil and lots of freshly ground black pepper.

Antipasto frittata

Serves 4

155 calories per serving

Takes 40 minutes +
5–10 minutes standing

Ⓥ

150 g (5½ oz) new potatoes

4 eggs

50 ml (2 fl oz) skimmed milk

1 tablespoon dried mixed
herbs

60 g (2 oz) roasted red
peppers in brine, drained,
de-seeded and sliced

25 g (1 oz) sliced black olives
in brine, drained

400 g can artichoke hearts in
brine, drained and halved

calorie controlled cooking
spray

salt and freshly ground black
pepper

Here are all the flavours of sunny Italy, wrapped up in a tasty wedge.

1 Bring a saucepan of water to the boil, add the potatoes and cook for 15–20 minutes. Drain, allow to cool enough to handle and then slice thinly.

2 Preheat the grill to medium. Whisk together the eggs, skimmed milk and dried herbs in a large bowl and season. Add the peppers, olives, artichoke hearts and potatoes, stirring until coated.

3 Heat a small, deep, non stick frying pan, ideally with a metal handle, spray with the cooking spray and pour in the eggs and vegetables. Using a spatula, flatten the top, distributing the vegetables. Gently cook for 5–6 minutes until golden underneath, transfer to the preheated grill and cook for 3–4 minutes until golden and just set. Put a cloth on the handle to remove the pan. Leave to stand for 5–10 minutes and then cut into four and serve.

Tip... If you don't have a metal handle on your frying pan, place the pan just far enough under the grill to cook the frittata.

Italian style poached egg

Serves 1
247 calories per serving
Takes 15 minutes

1 tablespoon white wine
  vinegar (optional)
1 egg
35 g (1¼ oz) slice ciabatta
15 g (½ oz) thin chorizo slices
15 g (½ oz) half fat Cheddar
  cheese, grated
freshly ground black pepper

*This Italian version of bacon and eggs with chorizo instead
of bacon truly hits the spot.*

1 Preheat the grill to hot. Bring a saucepan of water to the boil
and add the vinegar, if using. Break the egg into a mug and
set aside. Using a wooden spoon, swirl the water to create a
whirlpool and then quickly and carefully lower the mug into the
water and empty out the egg. Gently simmer for 3–4 minutes
until opaque and cooked. Remove from the saucepan with a
slotted spoon and drain on kitchen towel.

2 Meanwhile, put the ciabatta on a grill pan and cook for
1 minute until toasted. Remove from the grill and turn the
ciabatta over to toast the other side. Add the chorizo slices to
the grill pan and cook for 1 minute until the chorizo is crispy.

3 Put the ciabatta on a plate, top with the chorizo and then the
poached egg. Sprinkle over the cheese and season with black
pepper. Serve immediately.

Marinated roast pepper antipasto

Serves 2
106 calories per serving
Takes 35 minutes + cooling
Ⓥ

2 red peppers, de-seeded and halved

2 yellow or orange peppers, de-seeded and halved

calorie controlled cooking spray

4 garlic cloves, sliced thinly

1 teaspoon balsamic vinegar

a small bunch of fresh basil, torn

salt and freshly ground black pepper

A simple salad that can be eaten as a starter, accompaniment or just as a light meal.

1 Preheat the oven to Gas Mark 7/220°C/fan oven 200°C and place the peppers skin side up on a baking tray. Bake for 20–30 minutes, or until charred. Remove from the oven, wrap them in a plastic bag and leave until cool enough to handle.

2 Meanwhile, heat a non stick frying pan and spray with the cooking spray. Fry the garlic for a few seconds until golden.

3 Peel the skin from the peppers and slice the flesh. Place in a serving bowl with any cooking juices from the tray, the garlic, balsamic vinegar and basil. Season, toss together and serve.

Perfect pizzas

Pizza marinara

Serves 4

370 calories per serving

Takes 30 minutes to prepare
+ 10 minutes cooling,
20 minutes to cook

❄

300 g (10½ oz) pizza dough
mix

1 teaspoon plain flour, for
flouring

calorie controlled cooking
spray

1 small onion, sliced

1 garlic clove, crushed

225 g can chopped tomatoes

2 tablespoons tomato purée

1 teaspoon caster sugar

½ teaspoon dried oregano

50 g (1¾ oz) cooked peeled
prawns, defrosted if frozen

125 g (4½ oz) canned tuna in
brine, drained and flaked

1 green pepper, de-seeded and
cut into thin rings

25 g (1 oz) stoned black
olives, sliced

100 g (3½ oz) mozzarella light,
sliced thinly

freshly ground black pepper

'Marinara' usually refers to a dish containing seafood.
Here, a pizza is topped with prawns and tuna.

1 Preheat the oven to Gas Mark 6/200°C/fan oven 180°C.
Using warm water, make up the pizza base mix according to
the packet instructions and knead the dough for 5 minutes.

2 Dust a work surface with the flour and roll out the dough
to a 30 cm (12 inch) circle to form the pizza base. Place it on
a non stick baking tray and cover with a damp tea towel while
you prepare the topping.

3 Heat a small non stick saucepan and spray it with the
cooking spray. Add the onion and garlic to the pan and cook,
stirring occasionally, over a medium to low heat, until the onion
has softened but not browned.

4 Stir in the chopped tomatoes, tomato purée, sugar and
oregano and simmer for 10 minutes. Allow the mixture to cool
for 10 minutes and then spread it over the pizza base to within
1 cm (½ inch) of the edge.

5 Scatter the prawns, tuna, pepper rings and sliced olives over
the pizza and finally top with the mozzarella slices. Season with
black pepper.

6 Bake the pizza for 20 minutes and then cut it into quarters
to serve.

Variation... Try other vegetables on top of the pizza, such
as ribbons of courgettes, sliced mushrooms or fresh
tomatoes.

Gourmet pizza

Serves 2

429 calories per serving

Takes 15 minutes to prepare
+ 1 hour 10 minutes rising,
15 minutes to cook

❄ (pizza bases covered in
sauce only)

**150 g (5½ oz) plain flour,
1 tablespoon reserved
for rolling**

1 teaspoon fast action yeast

1 teaspoon olive oil

230 g can chopped tomatoes

1 small garlic clove, crushed

**1 tablespoon chopped fresh
basil**

**100 g (3½ oz) cherry
tomatoes, halved**

**80 g (3 oz) mozzarella light,
sliced**

**2 slices Parma ham, roughly
torn**

25 g (1 oz) wild rocket

**salt and freshly ground black
pepper**

*You can easily vary the basic pizza recipe here to add
your favourite toppings to the uncooked pizza. Allowing
the pizzas to rise before baking gives a thicker base that
doesn't dry out during cooking.*

1 Sift the flour into a mixing bowl. Stir in the yeast and
½ teaspoon of salt, make a well in the centre and add the olive
oil. Mix in around 100 ml (3½ fl oz) of warm water, or enough
to bring the mixture together to form a soft, but not sticky,
dough.

2 Turn out on to a floured surface and knead for 3 minutes until
smooth. Return to the bowl, cover with cling film and leave to
rise in a warm place for 1 hour, or until doubled in size.

3 Preheat the oven to Gas Mark 6/200°C/fan oven 180°C.
Place the chopped tomatoes, garlic and basil in a saucepan,
season, simmer briskly for 5 minutes until thickened and then
cool.

4 Divide the pizza dough into half and roll out two bases, each
measuring around 18 cm (7 inches) in diameter. Transfer to a non
stick baking tray (you may need two), spread with the tomato
sauce and then scatter the cherry tomatoes and mozzarella on
top. Leave to rise in a warm place for 10 minutes.

5 Bake the pizzas for 15 minutes until well risen and crisp. Top
with the torn Parma ham and rocket and serve immediately.

Pizza calzone

Serves 2
453 calories per serving
Takes 20 minutes to prepare +
1 hour rising, 10–12 minutes
to cook

Ⓥ

For the pizza dough
**175 g (6 oz) plain flour, plus
1 tablespoon for kneading**
1 teaspoon fast action yeast
½ teaspoon sugar
½ teaspoon salt
1 teaspoon olive oil

For the filling
100 g (3½ oz) Quark
**2 teaspoons Parmesan cheese,
grated**
**75 g (2¾ oz) pimientos in
brine, drained and sliced**
**1 tablespoon shredded fresh
basil**
3 tablespoons passata
**salt and freshly ground black
pepper**

*A calzone is a pizza that has been folded over to enclose
the filling – rather like a giant Cornish pasty. If you've
never tried making pizza dough before, do give it a go
as it really is very simple.*

1 Sift the flour into a mixing bowl and then stir in the yeast,
sugar and salt. Make a well in the centre, pour in the oil and
add enough warm water to bring the dough together – about
125 ml (4 fl oz).

2 Turn out on to a floured surface and knead for 3 minutes
until smooth. Return the dough to the bowl, cover with cling
film and leave to rise for 1 hour or until doubled in bulk.

3 Preheat the oven to Gas Mark 6/200°C/fan oven 180°C.

4 For the filling, mix the Quark and Parmesan together with
some seasoning. Mix the pimientos, basil and passata together.

5 Divide the dough ball in half and roll each out to an 18 cm
(7 inch) circle. Transfer to a baking tray.

6 Spread the Quark mixture over half of each dough circle and
top it with the pimento mixture. Moisten the edges with water,
fold the untopped dough over the filling and pinch the edges
to seal. Make a small hole in the top of each calzone.

7 Bake for 10–12 minutes until crisp and golden.

Tip... Make double the quantity of pizza dough and use to
roll out a 25 cm (10 inch) pizza base.

Variation... For a wonderful version with mushrooms,
spinach and ham, see the recipe on page 51.

Mushroom, spinach and ham calzone

Serves 2

388 calories per serving

Takes 20 minutes to prepare +
1 hour rising, 10–12 minutes
to cook

For the pizza dough

**175 g (6 oz) plain flour, plus
1 tablespoon for kneading**

1 teaspoon fast action yeast

½ teaspoon sugar

½ teaspoon salt

1 teaspoon olive oil

For the filling

**100 g (3½ oz) mushrooms,
sliced**

75 g (2¾ oz) spinach, washed

**60 g (2 oz) wafer thin ham,
sliced**

**1 tablespoon shredded fresh
basil**

3 tablespoons passata

**salt and freshly ground black
pepper**

Serve this unusual folded pizza with a crisp mixed salad.

1 Sift the flour into a mixing bowl and then stir in the yeast,
sugar and salt. Make a well in the centre, pour in the oil and
add enough warm water to bring the dough together – about
125 ml (4 fl oz).

2 Turn out on to a floured surface and knead for 3 minutes
until smooth. Return the dough to the bowl, cover with cling
film and leave to rise for 1 hour or until doubled in bulk.

3 Preheat the oven to Gas Mark 6/200°C/fan oven 180°C.

4 For the filling, heat a non stick pan and dry fry the mushrooms
until lightly browned. Add the spinach and cook until wilted.
Remove from the heat, mix in the ham and season. Mix the
basil and passata together.

5 Divide the dough ball in half and roll each out to an 18 cm
(7 inch) circle. Transfer to a baking tray.

6 Spread the spinach mixture over half of each dough circle
and top it with the passata mixture. Moisten the edges with
water, fold the untopped dough over the filling and pinch the
edges to seal. Make a small hole in the top of each calzone.

7 Bake for 10–12 minutes until crisp and golden.

ⓥ **Variation...** For a great vegetarian version, see the recipe
on page 49.

Artichoke and green olive pizza

Serves 2

451 calories per serving

Takes 15 minutes to prepare
 + 20 minutes rising,
 10–15 minutes to cook

Ⓥ

175 g (6 oz) strong white flour,
 plus 1 tablespoon for dusting

½ teaspoon fast action dried
 yeast

½ teaspoon sugar

½ teaspoon salt

1 teaspoon mixed dried herbs

2 vine ripened tomatoes,
 sliced

3 artichoke hearts in brine,
 drained and quartered

25 g (1 oz) stoned green olives
 in brine, drained and halved

40 g (1½ oz) half fat Cheddar
 cheese, grated

salt and freshly ground black
 pepper

a handful of fresh basil leaves,
 to garnish

*Get the kids to help make this pizza – they will enjoy
kneading the dough and eating their own handiwork.*

1 To make the base, place the flour, yeast, sugar and salt in a
bowl with the herbs and mix together. Add 125 ml (4 fl oz) of
hand hot water and mix to a dough.

2 Use half of the reserved flour to dust a work surface and
knead the dough for 5 minutes until smooth and elastic. Return
to the bowl and leave in a warm place for about 20 minutes
until doubled in size.

3 Preheat the oven to Gas Mark 6/200°C/fan oven 180°C.
Knock back the dough by punching it down. Use the remaining
flour to dust a work surface and then knead for a minute or so.

4 Divide the dough in two and roll each to a round approximately
15 cm (6 inches) in diameter. Place on a non stick baking tray.
Top with the sliced tomatoes, the artichokes and olives and
finally the cheese.

5 Season and bake for 10–15 minutes until the base is golden
and risen. Garnish with the fresh basil before serving.

Florentine pizza

Serves 2
350 calories per serving
Takes 30 minutes
Ⓥ

145 g packet pizza dough mix
300 g (10½ oz) spinach, washed
1 garlic clove, crushed
2 tablespoons tomato purée
2 eggs
salt and freshly ground black pepper

Placing the pizza dough in the oven for a short while helps it to rise more quickly and reduces the preparation time.

1 Preheat the oven to Gas Mark 7/220°C/fan oven 200°C.

2 Make up the dough according to the packet instructions, dividing it to make two pizzas. Roll out to circles of approximately 20 cm (8 inch) diameter and place on a baking tray (you may need two). Put in the oven for 2 minutes so that it begins to rise.

3 Cook the spinach in a steamer, or in a pan with 3 tablespoons of water, for 3–4 minutes until wilted. Drain well and, when cool enough to handle, squeeze out any excess water and chop roughly. Mix with the garlic and season.

4 Spread the tomato purée over the pizza bases and top with the spinach, making a well in the middle. Bake for 5 minutes and then remove from the oven. Crack an egg into the middle of each pizza, so that it is contained within the spinach, and bake for a further 8–10 minutes until the bases are crispy.

Tip... Eat hot or cool and then pack to enjoy for lunch.

Simple pastas

Lasagne

Serves 4

398 calories per serving

Takes 30 minutes to prepare,
45–50 minutes to cook

❄

300 g (10½ oz) extra lean beef
mince

1 onion, chopped

175 g (6 oz) mushrooms,
sliced

400 g can chopped tomatoes
with garlic

150 ml (5 fl oz) beef stock

2 teaspoons dried Italian
herbs

300 ml (10 fl oz) skimmed milk

3 tablespoons plain flour

1 tablespoon low fat spread

50 g (1¾ oz) half fat mature
Cheddar cheese, grated

110 g (4 oz) no precook
lasagne sheets

salt and freshly ground black
pepper

*Lasagne is one of the all-time favourite Italian dishes. Try
this healthier traditional version, it is full of great flavours.*

1 Preheat the oven to Gas Mark 5/190°C/fan oven 170°C.

2 Heat a large non stick pan and add the mince a handful at a
time, dry frying it until sealed and browned. Add the onion and
sauté for another 2–3 minutes, until the onion has softened.

3 Add the mushrooms, tomatoes, stock and herbs. Bring up to
the boil, reduce the heat and simmer for 15–20 minutes, until
reduced slightly. Remove from the heat and season to taste.

4 To make the sauce, put the milk, flour and low fat spread
into a non stick saucepan. Heat, stirring constantly with a small
wire whisk, until the mixture is thickened and smooth. Remove
from the heat and stir in most of the cheese. Season.

5 Spoon half the beef mixture into an oblong ovenproof dish.
Lay half the lasagne sheets on top. Spread 2–3 tablespoonfuls
of the cheese sauce over these sheets and top with the
remaining meat mixture. Lay the rest of the lasagne sheets
on top and then spread the rest of the sauce over the surface.
Sprinkle with the reserved cheese. Bake for 45–50 minutes
until golden brown and bubbling.

Tip... It's vital to use a proper measuring spoon when
meauring out the flour, otherwise the sauce will be too
thick.

Ⓥ Variation... For a wonderful vegetarian version, see the
recipe on page 75.

Pasta puttanesca

Serves 2
271 calories per serving
Takes 15 minutes

125 g (4½ oz) dried penne
calorie controlled cooking
  spray
1 garlic clove, crushed
a pinch of crushed dried
  chillies
1 tablespoon torn fresh basil,
  plus extra to garnish
1 tablespoon capers, drained
  and rinsed
10 black olives, stoned and
  chopped
1 teaspoon tomato purée
4 anchovy fillets, chopped
  (optional)
230 g can chopped tomatoes

*Puttanesca is a deliciously spicy and rustic Italian sauce,
full of gutsy flavours.*

1 Bring a saucepan of water to the boil, add the pasta and
cook according to the packet instructions. Drain, reserving
2 tablespoons of the cooking water.

2 Meanwhile, heat a non stick pan, spray with the cooking
spray and cook the garlic and crushed chillies for 30 seconds.
Add the remaining ingredients and simmer the sauce for
5 minutes.

3 Add the reserved cooking water to the sauce and then toss
with the pasta. Serve in warmed bowls, garnished with the
fresh basil.

 Variation... For a vegetarian alternative, simply leave out
the anchovies.

Spaghetti carbonara

Serves 2

385 calories per serving

Takes 10 minutes to prepare,
15 minutes to cook

110 g (4 oz) dried spaghetti
1 teaspoon olive oil
½ small onion, chopped finely
1 small garlic clove, peeled
and left whole
100 g (3½ oz) low fat soft
cheese
1 egg
5 tablespoons skimmed milk
25 g (1 oz) Parma ham or lean
boiled ham, cut into strips
15 g (½ oz) Parmesan cheese,
finely grated
2 teaspoons chopped fresh
oregano or parsley
salt and freshly ground black
pepper
fresh oregano or parsley
sprigs, to garnish

You can use spaghetti, fettuccine or tagliatelle to make this carbonara.

1 Bring a saucepan of water to the boil, add the pasta and cook for 12 minutes or according to the packet instructions.

2 Meanwhile, heat the oil in a non stick frying pan and sauté the onion and whole garlic clove for about 5 minutes, until softened. Discard the garlic clove.

3 Put the soft cheese in a bowl and beat with a wooden spoon to soften it. Add the egg and onion, stirring until combined. Add the milk, ham, Parmesan and the oregano or parsley, mix together and season.

4 Drain the pasta, reserving a couple of tablespoons of the cooking liquid, and then return it to the saucepan with the reserved liquid. Add the egg mixture and heat gently for 2–3 minutes, stirring, until the mixture has cooked and thickened.

5 Serve garnished with the sprigs of oregano or parsley.

Zesty seafood shells

Serves 2
428 calories per serving
Takes 35 minutes

125 g (4½ oz) dried large
pasta shells

calorie controlled cooking
spray

1 garlic clove, crushed

50 g (1¾ oz) baby spinach,
washed

4 vine ripened tomatoes,
de-seeded and diced

150 g (5½ oz) cooked seafood
medley (containing prawns,
squid and mussels),
defrosted if frozen

75 g (2¾ oz) cooked peeled
king prawns

4 tablespoons low fat plain
cottage cheese

grated zest of a lemon

salt and freshly ground black
pepper

*Serve with a large salad of mixed leaves, sweetcorn,
radishes, peppers and tomatoes.*

1 Bring a large saucepan of water to the boil, add the pasta
and cook for 10–12 minutes or according to the packet
instructions until 'al dente'. Drain and return to the pan.

2 Meanwhile, heat a large non stick frying pan and spray with
the cooking spray. Add the garlic, spinach, tomatoes, seafood
and prawns and heat gently for 5 minutes.

3 Add the cottage cheese, lemon zest and cooked pasta. Mix
together and heat through for a few minutes. Season and serve.

Spaghetti bolognese

Serves 4
382 calories per serving
Takes 40 minutes
❄ (sauce only)

**calorie controlled cooking
  spray**
**200 g (7 oz) extra lean beef
  mince**
2 onions, chopped finely
4 garlic cloves, chopped finely
2 tablespoons soy sauce
2 celery sticks, diced
2 carrots, peeled and diced
4 courgettes, chopped
**2 x 400 g cans chopped
  tomatoes**
**1 teaspoon dried oregano or
  Mediterranean herbs**
225 g (8 oz) dried spaghetti
**salt and freshly ground black
  pepper**

A simple and quick recipe for this favourite family meal.

1 Spray a large non stick frying pan with the cooking spray and put on a medium heat. Fry the mince with some seasoning, breaking it up with a wooden spoon or spatula until browned all over.

2 Add the onions and garlic and cook for about 5 minutes until softened, adding a splash of water if they start to stick.

3 Add the soy sauce, celery, carrots, courgettes, tomatoes and herbs and season. Stir and bring to the boil. Turn down the heat and simmer for 30 minutes.

4 Meanwhile, bring a saucepan of water to the boil, add the pasta and cook for 10 minutes or according to the packet instructions. Drain and serve with the sauce.

Savoury pasta slices

Serves 6

160 calories per serving

Takes 20 minutes to prepare + cooling, 30 minutes to cook

❄

calorie controlled cooking spray

a bunch of spring onions, chopped finely

90 g (3¼ oz) dried small pasta shapes

90 g (3¼ oz) lean cooked ham, chopped

90 g (3¼ oz) half fat mature Cheddar cheese, grated

3 eggs, beaten

1 tablespoon chopped fresh mixed herbs or 1 teaspoon dried herbs

salt and freshly ground black pepper

These slices are great hot or cold and perfect to pop in a picnic hamper.

1 Preheat the oven to Gas Mark 5/190°C/fan oven 170°C. Spray a 20 cm (8 inch) cake tin with the cooking spray.

2 Bring a small amount of water to the boil, add the spring onions and cook for 3–4 minutes.

3 At the same time, bring a second saucepan of water to the boil, add the pasta and cook for 8–10 minutes, until just tender. Drain the spring onions and pasta and set aside to cool slightly.

4 Mix together the spring onions, pasta, ham, cheese, eggs and herbs. Season well and then transfer to the prepared tin. Level the surface.

5 Bake for about 30 minutes until firm and golden. Allow to cool completely before removing from the tin and then cut into six wedges.

Tip... To keep for later, wrap the slices tightly in foil or greaseproof paper.

Caramelised tomato and pepper pasta

Serves 4
298 calories per serving
Takes 30 minutes
Ⓥ

1½ red peppers, de-seeded
and diced
1½ yellow peppers, de-seeded
and diced
calorie controlled cooking
spray
500 g (1 lb 2 oz) cherry
tomatoes, halved
3 garlic cloves, crushed
4 tablespoons shredded fresh
basil
250 g (9 oz) dried pasta shells
75 g (2¾ oz) low fat soft
cheese with garlic and herbs
freshly ground black pepper

Serve with a large mixed salad.

1 Preheat the oven to Gas Mark 7/220°C/fan oven 200°C.

2 Spread the peppers out on a large baking tray. Lightly spray with the cooking spray and then place in the oven on the top shelf for 15 minutes.

3 Place the tomatoes in a roasting tin, scatter with the garlic and 2 tablespoons of the basil and season with black pepper. Mist with the cooking spray and place in the oven below the peppers. Cook for 10 minutes. Stir both trays halfway through.

4 Bring a saucepan of water to the boil, add the pasta and cook for 10–12 minutes or according to the packet instructions. Drain.

5 Mix the pasta with the soft cheese, roasted peppers and remaining basil. Gently stir in the tomatoes and their juices and serve in warmed bowls.

Spaghetti with baby clams

Serves 4
456 calories per serving
Takes 25 minutes

350 g (12 oz) dried spaghetti
calorie controlled cooking
  spray
2 onions, chopped
4 garlic cloves, chopped
150 ml (5 fl oz) fish or
  vegetable stock
400 g can chopped tomatoes
1 teaspoon caster sugar
2 x 280 g cans baby clams,
  drained
2 teaspoons dried oregano
  or 1 packet fresh parsley,
  chopped
salt and freshly ground black
  pepper

*This dish makes a regular appearance on the menus of
restaurants all over Italy.*

1 Bring a saucepan of water to the boil, add the pasta and
cook according to the packet instructions. Drain, rinse and
keep warm.

2 Meanwhile, spray a large non stick frying pan or wok with
the cooking spray and put on a medium heat. Add the onions
and garlic and stir fry until softened.

3 Add the stock, tomatoes and sugar, season and cook for
15 minutes or until reduced by a third.

4 Add the clams and oregano or parsley. As soon as the clams
are heated through the sauce is ready. Pour over the spaghetti
and serve immediately.

Tip... Clams, called 'vongole', are available in cans and jars
from most supermarkets.

Variation... You can make this dish using 490 g (1 lb 2 oz)
of fresh mussels. First wash them under a running tap and
then remove the beards. Put them in a pan with the lid on
and, giving them an occasional shake, cook for 4 minutes
or until most of the shells have opened. Throw away any
that haven't opened. Remove the rest from their shells
ready to add to the sauce.

Pasta primavera

Serves 4
319 calories per serving
Takes 40 minutes

🅥
❄

225 g (8 oz) dried penne

calorie controlled cooking spray

a bunch of spring onions, chopped

100 g (3½ oz) fine asparagus spears, halved

1 courgette, chopped

75 g (2¾ oz) frozen petit pois or garden peas

100 g (3½ oz) very low fat plain fromage frais

250 g (9 oz) low fat soft cheese with garlic and herbs

finely grated zest of a lemon

a few fresh mint leaves, torn into shreds

20 g (¾ oz) Parmesan cheese, grated

salt and freshly ground black pepper

To garnish
a handful of fresh mint leaves
4 lemon wedges

Literally meaning 'springtime pasta', this classic Italian dish is bursting with the new season's flavours. Make sure that the vegetables are really fresh for the very best result.

1 Bring a saucepan of water to the boil, add the pasta and cook for about 8–10 minutes or according to the packet instructions, until just tender.

2 Meanwhile, lightly spray a large saucepan with the cooking spray and sauté the spring onions for about 3 minutes, until softened. Add the asparagus, courgette and petit pois or garden peas. Cook, stirring, for 2–3 minutes.

3 Add the fromage frais, soft cheese, lemon zest and torn mint leaves to the pan. Cook gently for about 4 minutes, stirring from time to time. Season.

4 Drain the pasta, reserving 2 tablespoons of the cooking liquid, and then return it with the reserved liquid to the saucepan. Add the sauce to the pasta, mixing it in gently.

5 Transfer the pasta mixture to four warmed plates and sprinkle each portion with 1 teaspoon of Parmesan cheese. Serve, garnished with mint leaves and a lemon wedge.

Tip... You don't have to use penne – any pasta shape will work well.

Variation... If asparagus is too expensive or not in season, use fine green beans instead.

Vegetarian lasagne

Serves 4

349 calories per serving

Takes 30 minutes to prepare,
45–50 minutes to cook

Ⓥ

❄

1 onion, chopped

350 g packet Quorn mince

175 g (6 oz) mushrooms,
sliced

400 g can chopped tomatoes
with garlic

150 ml (5 fl oz) vegetable
stock

2 teaspoons dried Italian
herbs

300 ml (10 fl oz) skimmed milk

3 tablespoons plain flour

1 tablespoon low fat spread

50 g (1¾ oz) half fat mature
Cheddar cheese, grated

110 g (4 oz) no precook
lasagne sheets

salt and freshly ground black
pepper

*Quorn mince can be used in place of beef mince in many
recipes. Here, it makes the perfect lasagne.*

1 Preheat the oven to Gas Mark 5/190°C/fan oven 170°C.

2 Heat a large non stick pan, add the onion and sauté for
2–3 minutes, until the onion has softened, adding a splash of
water if it starts to stick.

3 Add the Quorn mince, mushrooms, tomatoes, stock and
herbs. Bring up to the boil, reduce the heat and simmer for
15–20 minutes, until reduced slightly. Remove from the heat
and season to taste.

4 To make the sauce, put the milk, flour and low fat spread
into a non stick saucepan. Heat, stirring constantly with a small
wire whisk, until the mixture is thickened and smooth. Remove
from the heat and stir in most of the cheese. Season.

5 Spoon half the Quorn mixture into an oblong ovenproof dish.
Lay half the lasagne sheets on top. Spread 2–3 tablespoonfuls
of the cheese sauce over these sheets and top with the
remaining Quorn mixture. Lay the rest of the lasagne sheets
on top and then spread the rest of the sauce over the surface.
Sprinkle with the reserved cheese.

6 Bake for 45–50 minutes until golden brown and bubbling.

Variation... For a meaty version, see the recipe on page 58.

Orecchiette with pork ragù

Serves 4
451 calories per serving
Takes 35 minutes
❄ (ragù sauce only)

500 g (1 lb 2 oz) extra lean pork mince
2 large garlic cloves, crushed
½ teaspoon fennel seeds
¼ teaspoon dried chilli flakes
1 tablespoon chopped fresh rosemary or 1 teaspoon dried rosemary
500 g jar passata
225 g (8 oz) dried orecchiette (or any other pasta shape)
225 g (8 oz) broccoli, cut into small florets
50 g (1¾ oz) very low fat plain fromage frais
salt and freshly ground black pepper

Fennel seeds and chilli are key flavouring ingredients in traditional Italian sausages, which are often used for rich pasta sauces like this one. Shaped pasta such as orecchiette, which literally translates as 'little ears', catches the meat sauce so that it doesn't fall to the bottom of your bowl.

1 In a large, lidded, non stick frying pan, dry fry the pork mince for 5 minutes, over a high heat, to brown. Add the garlic, fennel seeds, chilli flakes and rosemary and cook for 1 minute.

2 Stir in the passata, season, cover and simmer for 30 minutes.

3 Meanwhile, bring a saucepan of water to the boil, add the pasta and cook according to the packet instructions, adding the broccoli for the last 3 minutes of the cooking time. Drain, reserving 100 ml (3½ fl oz) of the cooking water.

4 Toss the pasta and broccoli with the sauce and stir in the fromage frais and reserved cooking water. Serve immediately In deep warmed bowls.

Creamy smoked mackerel pasta

Serves 4

543 calories per serving

Takes 15 minutes

This is a simple fast dish that tastes absolutely delicious. Serve with a selection of seasonal steamed vegetables, if you wish.

240 g (8½ oz) dried pasta

325 g (11½ oz) smoked mackerel, flaked

4 tablespoons half fat crème fraîche

25 g packet fresh parsley, chopped

salt and freshly ground black pepper

1 Bring a saucepan of water to the boil, add the pasta and cook according to the packet instructions or until tender. Drain.

2 Toss the pasta with the other ingredients and serve immediately in warmed bowls.

Lentil and pasta bolognese

Serves 4

399 calories per serving

Takes 10 minutes to prepare,
50 minutes to cook

Ⓥ

❄ (bolognese only)

calorie controlled cooking
spray

1 red onion, diced

1 red pepper, de-seeded and
diced

1 courgette, diced

2 garlic cloves, crushed

200 g (7 oz) dried Puy lentils

700 g jar passata with herbs

300 ml (10 fl oz) vegetable
stock

250 g (9 oz) dried spaghetti or
tagliatelle

30 g (1¼ oz) Parmesan
cheese, grated, to serve

Non-vegetarians will really enjoy this tasty pasta dish too.

1 Spray a large non stick pan with the cooking spray and heat until hot. Add the onion, pepper, courgette and garlic and stir fry for 5 minutes until softened, adding a splash of water if they start to stick.

2 Add the lentils, passata and stock. Bring to the boil and simmer for 15 minutes until the lentils are tender.

3 Meanwhile, bring a large saucepan of water to the boil, add the pasta and cook for 10–12 minutes or according to the packet instructions. Drain.

4 Divide the pasta between four warmed plates, top with the bolognese sauce and sprinkle the Parmesan over.

Seafood lasagne

Serves 6

258 calories per serving

Takes 15 minutes to prepare,
40–50 minutes to cook

**calorie controlled cooking
spray**

2 leeks, sliced finely

**500 g (1 lb 2 oz) cooked mixed
seafood (e.g. squid, mussels,
prawns), defrosted if frozen**

50 ml (2 fl oz) white wine

**1 fish or vegetable stock cube,
crumbled**

15 g (½ oz) low fat spread

15 g (½ oz) plain flour

600 ml (20 fl oz) skimmed milk

25 g packet fresh dill, chopped

**150 g (5½ oz) no precook
lasagne sheets**

1 egg, beaten

8 cherry tomatoes, halved

**25 g (1 oz) half fat mature
Cheddar cheese, grated**

**salt and freshly ground black
pepper**

*Italians love seafood, so why not combine it with a
traditional Italian dish in this tasty lasagne.*

1 Preheat the oven to Gas Mark 5/190°C/fan oven 170°C.
Spray a large non stick frying pan with the cooking spray and
heat until hot. Add the leeks and stir fry for 5 minutes until
softened. Add the seafood, wine and stock cube and heat
through for a few minutes. Remove from the heat.

2 To make the sauce, melt the low fat spread in a small pan
and stir in the flour. Cook for 1 minute and then remove from
the heat. Add the milk a little at a time, stirring to a smooth
paste each time before adding more. Stir in the dill and season.

3 Pour half the sauce (reserving the other half) into the
seafood mixture and stir well. Spoon half of this mixture into
a 25 cm (10 inch) square ovenproof dish. Top with half of the
lasagne sheets, the remaining seafood mixture and the rest
of the lasagne sheets.

4 Beat the egg into the reserved sauce and spread over the
top of the lasagne. Scatter over the tomatoes and sprinkle over
the cheese. Place on a baking tray and bake for 40–50 minutes
until cooked through and golden on top.

Creamy chicken pasta

Serves 4

438 calories per serving

Takes 15 minutes to prepare,
20 minutes to cook

1 tablespoon plain flour

330 g (11½ oz) skinless
boneless chicken breasts,
cut into chunks

2 tablespoons olive oil

225 g (8 oz) dried tagliatelle

100 g (3½ oz) mange tout,
sliced

1 courgette, chopped

300 ml (10 fl oz) skimmed milk

1 chicken or vegetable stock
cube

1 teaspoon dried Italian herbs

2 tomatoes, skinned and finely
chopped

salt and freshly ground black
pepper

To serve

1 tablespoon finely grated
Parmesan cheese

fresh basil sprigs

Try this summery pasta dish for a quick and simple supper.

1 Sprinkle the flour on a plate and season. Roll the chicken pieces in this mixture.

2 Heat the olive oil in a large non stick frying pan and add the chicken pieces. Cook for about 6–8 minutes, turning often, until brown.

3 Meanwhile, bring a saucepan of water to the boil, add the pasta and cook for about 8 minutes, until tender. At the same time, cook the mange tout with the courgette in a little water for about 5 minutes.

4 Add the milk, stock cube and herbs to the chicken and stir until just boiling. Reduce the heat and cook gently for 2–3 minutes, stirring often.

5 Drain the pasta and the vegetables and toss them together with the tomatoes. Add the chicken mixture and stir together gently. Season to taste and then serve, sprinkled with the Parmesan cheese and garnished with the basil.

Variations... Use your choice of pasta shapes instead of tagliatelle, and use shavings of Parmesan cheese instead of grated.

Ⓥ For a vegetarian version, use 225 g (8 oz) of smoked tofu pieces instead of chicken.

Mushroom and ricotta cannelloni

Serves 4
336 calories per serving
Takes 35 minutes to prepare,
25 minutes to cook

Ⓥ
❄

calorie controlled cooking
spray
1 red onion, chopped
1 garlic clove, crushed
450 g (1 lb) mushrooms,
chopped finely
200 g (7 oz) baby spinach,
washed
a pinch of grated nutmeg
200 g (7 oz) ricotta
225 g (8 oz) no precook
cannelloni tubes
400 g can chopped tomatoes
with herbs
150 ml (5 fl oz) passata
salt and freshly ground black
pepper

Try using a mixture of mushrooms such as button, oyster and shiitake to add extra flavour to the finished dish.

1 Heat a non stick frying pan and spray it with the cooking spray. Add the onion, garlic and mushrooms and cook for 5 minutes until softened. Add the spinach and nutmeg and cook for a few more minutes until the spinach wilts.

2 Remove the pan from the heat, season to taste and beat in the ricotta. Preheat the oven to Gas Mark 5/190°C/fan oven 170°C.

3 Pack the spinach and ricotta filling into the cannelloni tubes and then arrange them in a shallow ovenproof dish.

4 Mix the chopped tomatoes with the passata and pour this over the cannelloni. Bake for 25 minutes.

Tip... The easiest way to fill the cannelloni tubes is with a small teaspoon, but cover the other end of the shell with your hand, being careful not to burn yourself, to prevent the filling falling out.

Variation... If you prefer, you can use eight cooked lasagne sheets to wrap around the filling, instead of cannelloni tubes.

Crab linguine

Serves 4
245 calories per serving
Takes 15 minutes

250 g (9 oz) dried linguine
170 g can crab meat in brine, drained
1 small red chilli, de-seeded and diced
2 spring onions, chopped
salt and freshly ground black pepper

To serve
3 tablespoons chopped fresh parsley
1 lime, cut into wedges

This is so simple to make, but it's very effective and tasty too.

1 Bring a large saucepan of water to the boil, add the pasta and cook according to the packet instructions. Drain well.

2 Stir in the crab meat, chilli and spring onions. Season and serve garnished with the parsley and with the lime wedge to squeeze over.

Supper dishes

Lemon chicken and chicory

Serves 4
133 calories per serving
Takes 45 minutes

calorie controlled cooking
  spray
2 garlic cloves, crushed
4 x 100 g (3½ oz) skinless
  boneless chicken breasts
grated zest and juice of a
  lemon
8 heads of chicory, each cut
  in half lengthways with the
  bitter end core scooped out
250 ml (9 fl oz) vegetable
  stock
a small bunch of fresh parsley,
  chopped roughly
200 g (7 oz) cherry tomatoes,
  quartered
salt and freshly ground black
  pepper

An easy one pot meal with lovely sharp clean flavours.

1 Preheat the oven to Gas Mark 4/180°C/fan oven 160°C.
Heat a large, lidded, flameproof and ovenproof casserole dish
and spray it with the cooking spray.

2 Fry the garlic for a few seconds and then add the chicken
breasts. Season and squeeze over the lemon juice. Allow the
chicken to brown all over before removing to a plate.

3 Spray the casserole dish again with the cooking spray and
fry the chicory on its cut side. Season and turn them until they
are browned all over. Pour over the stock and then lay the
chicken on top.

4 Scatter over half the parsley and the lemon zest, cover and
put in the oven to cook for 35 minutes or until the chicken is
cooked through and the chicory is tender.

5 Season the tomatoes in a small bowl and mix with the
remaining parsley before scattering them over the chicken
and chicory. Serve immediately.

Mediterranean roasted steak

Serves 2
494 calories per serving
Takes 25 minutes

200 g (7 oz) baby new
  potatoes, peeled and cut into
  small cubes

calorie controlled cooking
  spray

2 x 200 g (7 oz) lean beef
  rump steaks, visible fat
  removed

400 g can chopped tomatoes

2 teaspoons Worcestershire
  sauce

½ tablespoon fresh oregano
  leaves

390 g can artichoke hearts in
  water, drained

10 black olives in brine,
  drained and halved

½ teaspoon paprika

salt and freshly ground black
  pepper

*Serve with 2 heaped tablespoons of cooked peas per
person and green beans.*

1 Preheat the oven to Gas Mark 6/200°C/fan oven 180°C
and put a shallow roasting tin in the oven to heat.

2 Put the potatoes in a bowl and microwave on high for
3 minutes. Transfer to the preheated roasting tin and spray
with the cooking spray. Bake in the oven for 5 minutes.

3 Meanwhile, heat a non stick frying pan and spray the steaks
with the cooking spray. Cook the steaks for 1 minute on each
side until browned. Transfer to a board.

4 Add the tomatoes and Worcestershire sauce to the frying
pan and bring to the boil. Bubble for 2–3 minutes until reduced
and thick. Season and stir in the oregano.

5 Remove the potatoes from the oven and stir in the tomato
sauce. Top with the artichoke hearts, olives and steaks.
Sprinkle over the paprika and bake for a further 10 minutes
until the steaks are medium rare. If you like them well done,
cook for 3–5 minutes longer. Serve immediately.

Tip... If you can't find fresh oregano, you can use dried
instead and simply stir in 1 teaspoon at the end of step 2.

Grilled trout with fennel

Serves 4
236 calories per serving
Takes 20 minutes

**2 large fennel bulbs, each
sliced into 6 lengthways**
**calorie controlled cooking
spray**
4 x 150 g (5½ oz) trout fillets
juice of a lemon
**salt and freshly ground black
pepper**

To serve
2 teaspoons olive oil
lemon wedges

*Fennel has a crisp aniseed flavour that complements the
oily trout. This is a light dish best served with a 50 g (1¾ oz)
crusty roll per person to mop up the juices.*

1 Preheat the grill to medium. Bring a saucepan of water to
the boil and boil or steam the fennel pieces for 5 minutes.

2 Spray an ovenproof dish with the cooking spray and lay the
fennel in it.

3 Season the trout fillets and place them on top of the fennel.
Pour the lemon juice over and spray with the cooking spray.

4 Grill for 8 minutes and then serve drizzled with the olive oil
and accompanied by the lemon wedges.

Italian stuffed pancakes

Serves 4
406 calories per serving
Takes 50 minutes to prepare, 30 minutes to cook

ⓥ
❄

For the filling
225 g (8 oz) potatoes, peeled
1 teaspoon vegetable oil
1 onion, chopped
2 garlic cloves, crushed
1 small leek, chopped
225 g (8 oz) frozen spinach, defrosted and
  squeezed
225 g (8 oz) ricotta
a pinch of grated nutmeg
salt and freshly ground black pepper

For the pancakes
110 g (4 oz) plain flour
a pinch of salt
1 egg
300 ml (3½ fl oz) skimmed milk
2 teaspoons vegetable oil

For the topping
1 tablespoon olive oil
1 small onion, chopped
400 g can chopped tomatoes with herbs
25 g (1 oz) half fat Cheddar cheese, grated

*These pancakes are perfect served with an assortment of steamed vegetables or a crisp
green salad.*

1 Bring a saucepan of water to the boil, add the potatoes and cook for 10 minutes. Drain, allow to
cool slightly and then dice.

2 Meanwhile, to make the pancakes, sift the flour and salt into a bowl and then make a well in the
centre. Break the egg into the well and then beat it in with a wooden spoon. Gradually beat in the
milk, drawing the flour in from the sides to make a smooth batter.

continues overleaf ▶

3 Heat an 18 cm (7 inch) non stick frying pan. Dip a piece of kitchen towel in the oil and wipe it around the pan to grease it lightly. Pour in just enough batter to coat the base of the pan thinly. Cook for 1–2 minutes, until the pancake is golden. Turn or toss the pancake over and cook the second side until golden. Transfer it to a plate and then repeat the process with the remaining batter, greasing the pan each time, to make eight pancakes. Stack them, interleaved with non stick baking parchment as you go. Preheat to oven to Gas Mark 6/200°C/fan oven 180°C.

4 To make the filling, heat the oil in a non stick frying pan, add the onion, garlic and leek and gently cook until softened. Stir in the spinach and cook for 1 minute. Remove the pan from the heat and then stir in the potatoes, ricotta and nutmeg. Season to taste.

5 To make the topping, heat the oil in a small pan and sauté the onion until soft. Add the tomatoes and cook for 5 minutes. If you want a smooth sauce, put the mixture in a blender, or use a hand held blender, and whizz until smooth.

6 Divide the filling equally between the pancakes, spooning it across one end. Roll up the pancakes and then arrange them, with the opening underneath, in a shallow ovenproof dish. Pour the topping over and then sprinkle with the Cheddar cheese.

7 Bake the pancakes for 30 minutes or until the topping bubbles. Serve immediately.

Tip... The pancake batter ingredients can be mixed together in a food processor or blender. Put the egg and liquid in first and then add the flour and whizz until smooth.

Squash and barley risotto

Serves 1

365 calories per serving

Takes 10 minutes to prepare, 40 minutes to cook

Ⓥ

calorie controlled cooking spray

200 g (7 oz) butternut squash, peeled, de-seeded and chopped into 5 cm (2 inch) dice

1 small onion, diced

500 ml (18 fl oz) vegetable stock

1 small garlic clove, crushed

a pinch of ground coriander

60 g (2 oz) dried pearl barley

salt and freshly ground black pepper

25 g (1 oz) rocket, to serve

Barley makes a lovely nutty alternative to rice in this delicious risotto. If you like, serve crumbled with 15 g (½ oz) of Stilton cheese.

1 Spray a non stick frying pan with the cooking spray and heat until hot. Add the squash and onion and pan fry for 5 minutes, adding a tablespoon of stock if they start to stick. Add the garlic and coriander and cook for a further minute.

2 Stir in the barley followed by a ladleful of stock. Reduce the heat to a low simmer, stirring regularly and letting all the stock be absorbed before adding another ladleful. Continue until all the stock has been used and the barley is tender. This will take about 25–35 minutes. Season and serve topped with the rocket.

Turkey scallopine with lemon and caper sauce

Serves 2
296 calories per serving
Takes 15 minutes

2 x 125 g (4½ oz) turkey breast steaks

grated zest and juice of ½ a small lemon

calorie controlled cooking spray

1 garlic clove, crushed

150 ml (5 fl oz) chicken stock

2 tablespoons chopped fresh parsley

1 tablespoon capers, drained and rinsed

salt and freshly ground black pepper

Serve with broccoli and 100 g (3½ oz) of potatoes, cooked and mashed with 1 tablespoon of skimmed milk per person.

1 Place each turkey steak between two layers of cling film and flatten out to about 5 mm (¼ inch) thick, using a rolling pin or heavy based pan. Press the lemon zest and seasoning into the steaks.

2 Heat a non stick frying pan, lightly spray with the cooking spray and fry the turkey steaks for 2½ minutes on each side. Move to a plate and keep warm.

3 Add the garlic to the pan and fry for a few seconds, without burning. Pour in the chicken stock and lemon juice and bubble fast for 3 minutes until the sauce has reduced by about half.

4 Stir in the parsley and capers and pour the sauce over the turkey. Serve immediately.

Eggs Florentine

Serves 4
259 calories per serving
Takes 20 minutes to prepare,
20 minutes to cook

Ⓥ

400 g (14 oz) frozen spinach
a pinch of grated nutmeg
500 ml (18 fl oz) vegetable
stock
4 large eggs
30 g (1¼ oz) butter
2 tablespoons plain flour
200 ml (7 fl oz) semi skimmed
milk
15 g (½ oz) Parmesan cheese,
grated
salt and freshly ground black
pepper

*Eggs Florentine is a traditional Italian dish made with
creamy spinach and topped with a poached egg.*

1 Heat the frozen spinach in a saucepan and add the nutmeg
and seasoning. Drain well and then spoon this over the base of
a shallow ovenproof dish.

2 Meanwhile, put the vegetable stock in a saucepan and bring
to the boil. Reduce to a gentle simmer. One by one, break the
eggs into a cup and slide them into the stock. Leave to poach
for 2–3 minutes.

3 Melt the butter in a small saucepan and then take it off the
heat. Stir in the flour to make a smooth paste. Place the pan
back on the heat and gradually add the milk and 2 tablespoons
of the vegetable stock from the other pan. Stir or whisk
continuously until it comes to the boil and you have a smooth
thick roux sauce. Season well. Pour two thirds of the sauce
over the spinach and gently mix it in.

4 Using a slotted spoon, remove the eggs from the saucepan
and place them on top of the spinach. Pour over the remaining
white sauce.

5 Preheat the grill to medium-high. Sprinkle the top of the dish
with the Parmesan and place it under the grill for 5–6 minutes
until golden and bubbling. Serve immediately.

Tip... When making a roux sauce do not be tempted to do
anything else – it needs to be stirred constantly to prevent
lumps.

Variation... For a tasty chicken version of this recipe, go to
page 118.

Lamb chops with Italian potatoes

Serves 4

529 calories per serving

Takes 10 minutes to prepare,
10–12 minutes to cook

**calorie controlled cooking
spray**

**450 g (1 lb) new potatoes,
scrubbed and diced**

12 cherry tomatoes, halved

**75 g (2¾ oz) stoned black
olives in brine, drained and
halved**

110 g (4 oz) spinach, washed

**8 x 75 g (2¾ oz) lamb chops,
visible fat removed**

**salt and freshly ground black
pepper**

*Serve with steamed green vegetables for a delicious meal
for all family and friends.*

1 Preheat the grill to medium. Spray a large non stick frying
pan with the cooking spray and heat until hot. Add the potatoes
and stir fry for 10–15 minutes until tender, adding a splash of
water if they start to stick. Add the tomatoes and olives and
cook for a minute before adding the spinach. Toss the mixture
for a minute or so, until the spinach just starts to wilt. Season.

2 Meanwhile, season the chops on both sides and then grill
for 10–12 minutes, turning once until just cooked through.

3 Serve the lamb chops on top of the potatoes.

✆ **Variation...** You can replace the lamb with a 250 g
packet of Quorn sausages, grilled according to the packet
instructions.

Chicken cacciatore

Serves 2
410 calories per serving
Takes 10 minutes to prepare, 1 hour to cook
❄ (chicken and sauce only)

200 g (7 oz) new potatoes
1 teaspoon olive oil
275 g (9½ oz) chicken legs, skinless
1 heaped tablespoon plain flour
1 large onion, chopped
1 garlic clove, crushed
400 g can chopped tomatoes

100 ml (3½ fl oz) chicken stock
1 teaspoon dried basil
150 g (5½ oz) mushrooms, sliced
calorie controlled cooking spray
salt and freshly ground black pepper
fresh basil leaves, to garnish (optional)

The mushroom and tomato sauce used in this recipe tastes fantastic and any leftovers make a great pasta sauce for the next day.

1 Bring a saucepan of water to the boil, add the potatoes and cook for 8–10 minutes. Drain, allow to cool and then cut into 5 mm (¼ inch) thick slices. Set aside.

2 Meanwhile, heat the oil over a medium-high heat in a large, lidded, non stick frying pan. Roll the chicken legs in the flour, season and brown them in the pan for 2 minutes on each side until golden. Reserve any remaining flour. Remove the chicken from the pan and set aside.

3 Fry the onion and garlic in the pan for 2–3 minutes or until they start to soften and change colour. Add a splash of water if necessary to prevent them from sticking.

continues overleaf ▶

4 Add the tomatoes, stock, basil and seasoning. Mix well and stir in any reserved flour. Add the chicken to the mixture, reduce the heat and cover the pan. Simmer for 20 minutes, stirring once or twice.

5 Add the mushrooms, making sure they are below the surface of the sauce, replace the lid and cook for a further 20 minutes.

6 Spray another non stick frying pan or wok with the cooking spray and add the sliced new potatoes. Fry for 10–15 minutes, turning them occasionally to brown them on both sides. Keep warm until ready to serve.

7 At the end of this time, check that the chicken is fully cooked and that the seasoning and the thickness of the sauce are to your liking. (You can thicken the sauce by simmering it uncovered for another 5 minutes, or thin it by adding a little water.)

8 Serve the chicken and sauce with the sauté potatoes, garnished with the fresh basil, if using.

Tip... When planning to serve sauté potatoes, you could boil the new potatoes in advance. They keep very well in the fridge for a day or two.

Variation... Chicken cacciatore is also wonderful served with 40 g (1½ oz) of dried pasta per person, cooked according to the packet instructions, instead of the potatoes.

Mediterranean butter beans

Serves 4

134 calories per serving

Takes 50 minutes to prepare
  + overnight soaking,
  45 minutes to cook

Ⓥ

❄

**150 g (5½ oz) dried butter
  beans (see Tip)**

**calorie controlled cooking
  spray**

2 onions, sliced

2 garlic cloves, crushed

2 courgettes, sliced

150 ml (5 fl oz) red wine

**2 x 400 g cans chopped
  tomatoes**

**1 vegetable stock cube,
  crumbled**

1 tablespoon dried oregano

**salt and freshly ground black
  pepper**

*Often enjoyed as a side dish, this is a great recipe in its
own right. Serve with a 50 g (1¾ oz) chunk of wholemeal
bread per person.*

1 Place the beans in a large saucepan, cover with cold water
and leave overnight to soak.

2 The next day, drain the beans, rinse and cover again with
water. Place the pan on the hob and bring the water to the
boil. Boil for 10 minutes and then reduce the heat and simmer
for 30 minutes. Drain and rinse. Set aside.

3 Rinse out the pan, spray with the cooking spray and heat
until hot. Add the onion and cook for 3–5 minutes until softened,
adding a splash of water if it begins to stick.

4 Add the garlic and courgettes, cook for another 3 minutes
and then add the wine. It will sizzle up and almost disappear.

5 Return the beans to the pan along with the tomatoes, stock
cube and oregano. Bring to the boil and simmer gently for
45 minutes until thickened. Season before serving.

Tip... In this recipe, dried butter beans are better than
canned ones because they thicken the dish and absorb
more flavour. But if you don't have time to soak them,
simply omit step 1 completely, add two 400 g cans of
butter beans, drained, in step 2, and decrease the
simmering time to 30 minutes.

Italian haddock bake

Serves 4
217 calories per serving
Takes 15 minutes to prepare,
40–45 minutes to cook

2 mixed peppers, de-seeded
and sliced
1 red onion, chopped roughly
2 garlic cloves, sliced
1 fennel bulb, diced roughly
calorie controlled cooking
spray
100 g (3½ oz) low fat soft
cheese
1 tablespoon chopped fresh
dill
15 g (½ oz) capers in brine,
drained and chopped finely
30 g (1¼ oz) gherkins, diced
finely
4 x 150 g (5½ oz) skinless
haddock loin fillets
1 tablespoon dried Italian
herbs
150 g (5½ oz) cherry
tomatoes, halved
185 g can pitted black olives
in brine, drained
freshly ground black pepper

This is a simple way to cook fish and vegetables.

1 Preheat the oven to Gas Mark 6/200°C/fan oven 180°C.
Put the peppers, onion, garlic and fennel in a shallow roasting
tin and spray with the cooking spray. Roast in the oven for
30 minutes, stirring the vegetables halfway through.

2 Meanwhile, in a small bowl, mix together the soft cheese,
dill, capers and gherkins and season with freshly ground black
pepper. Lay the haddock fillets on a board and generously
spread one side of each fillet with the soft cheese mixture.
Set aside.

3 Remove the vegetables from the oven and stir in the dried
herbs. Scatter over the tomatoes and olives and lay the haddock
fillets on top of the vegetables, leaving a little gap between
each fish fillet. Bake in the oven for a further 10–15 minutes
until cooked and golden. Serve immediately.

Sun drenched turkey towers

Serves 4
222 calories per serving
Takes 40 minutes

4 x 100 g (3½ oz) turkey
  breast steaks, each sliced
  into four even sized
  medallions
grated zest and juice of a
  lemon
1 garlic clove, crushed
1 teaspoon olive oil
2 tablespoons pesto sauce
2 tablespoons boiling water
2 aubergines, cut into 16
  slices about 5 mm (¼ inch)
  thick
4 large beef tomatoes, cut
  into 16 slices about 5 mm
  (¼ inch) thick
2 yellow peppers, de-seeded
  and quartered
salt and freshly ground black
  pepper
fresh basil leaves, to garnish

You really need a griddle pan or barbecue to make these.

1 Put the turkey steaks on a large plate and season. Mix together the lemon zest and juice, garlic and olive oil and pour over the turkey.

2 Preheat a griddle pan so it's really hot. Mix the pesto sauce and boiling water together and brush the aubergine and tomato slices with the mixture.

3 Char the turkey steaks on both sides on the griddle and then turn down the heat and cook them for about 2 minutes more, until cooked through. Remove from the heat and set aside but keep warm.

4 Get the griddle really hot again and then char all the vegetables on both sides, brushing with more pesto sauce as you go. As they are done, remove from the heat and set aside but keep warm.

5 To serve, place a slice of aubergine on each plate and top with a piece of turkey, a slice of tomato and a slice of pepper. Repeat the layers to make a tower and serve two towers on each plate, scattered with the basil.

Pesto chicken

Serves 2

288 calories per serving

Takes 15 minutes to prepare,
   30 minutes to cook

❄

2 x 150 g (5½ oz) skinless
   boneless chicken breasts

4 large fresh basil leaves

1 tablespoon pesto sauce

75 g (2¾ oz) low fat soft
   cheese

1 beefsteak tomato, sliced

1 tablespoon grated Parmesan
   cheese

salt and freshly ground black
   pepper

*A tasty and easy way to add Italian flavour to a simple
chicken breast.*

1 Preheat the oven to Gas Mark 5/190°C/fan oven 170°C.

2 Make a slit along the length of each chicken breast and
push two basil leaves into each slit.

3 Beat together the pesto and soft cheese and spread this
mixture on top of each chicken breast. Season and then lay
the chicken in a shallow ovenproof dish. Top with a layer of
tomato slices.

4 Sprinkle the Parmesan cheese over the top and bake in the
oven for 30 minutes. Serve hot.

Aubergine parmigiana

Serves 2

234 calories per serving

Takes 30 minutes to prepare,
20–25 minutes to cook

Ⓥ

**1 yellow pepper, de-seeded
and quartered**

**1 large courgette, cut into
1 cm (½ inch) slices**

**calorie controlled cooking
spray**

**1 aubergine, cut into 1 cm
(½ inch) slices**

400 g can chopped tomatoes

grated zest of a lemon

**1 tablespoon shredded fresh
basil**

**125 g (4½ oz) mozzarella light,
sliced thinly**

**15 g (½ oz) Parmesan cheese,
grated**

**salt and freshly ground black
pepper**

This tasty recipe exudes the flavours of the Mediterranean.

1 Preheat the grill to its highest setting and place the pepper and courgette slices on the grill tray. Lightly spray with the cooking spray and place under the grill. Grill the courgette slices for 5 minutes on each side until golden. Grill the peppers for 8–10 minutes until the skins are charred.

2 Transfer the courgettes to a plate. Place the peppers in a bowl, cover, leave to cool and then peel off the skins.

3 Place the aubergine slices on the grill pan, spray with the cooking spray and grill for 3–4 minutes on each side until browned.

4 Meanwhile, preheat the oven to Gas Mark 6/200°C/fan oven 180°C. Make the tomato sauce by simmering the tomatoes, lemon zest and basil for 6–8 minutes until slightly thickened. Season.

5 Spread half the tomato sauce in the base of a small ovenproof baking dish and lay half of the aubergines on top. Cover with the courgettes and peppers, add the remaining aubergines and tomato sauce, followed by the sliced mozzarella and grated Parmesan. Bake for 20–25 minutes until bubbling.

Chicken Florentine

Serves 4

335 calories per serving

Takes 25 minutes to prepare,
20 minutes to cook

500 ml (18 fl oz) chicken stock

4 x 165 g (6 oz) skinless
boneless chicken breasts

400 g (14 oz) frozen spinach

a pinch of grated nutmeg

30 g (1¼ oz) butter

2 tablespoons plain flour

200 ml (7 fl oz) semi skimmed
milk

15 g (½ oz) Parmesan cheese,
grated

salt and freshly ground black
pepper

*In this version of eggs Florentine, the spinach is topped
with chicken.*

1 Put the chicken stock in a saucepan and bring to the boil.
Add the chicken and poach for 15 minutes.

2 Meanwhile, heat the frozen spinach in a saucepan and add
the nutmeg and seasoning. Drain well and then spoon this over
the base of a shallow ovenproof dish.

3 Melt the butter in a small saucepan and then take it off the
heat. Stir in the flour to make a smooth paste. Place the pan
back on the heat and gradually add the milk and 2 tablespoons
of the chicken stock from the other pan. Stir or whisk
continuously until it comes to the boil and you have a smooth
thick roux sauce. Season well.

4 Pour two thirds of the sauce over the spinach and gently
mix it in.

5 Using a slotted spoon, remove the chicken breasts from the
saucepan and place them on top of the spinach. Pour over the
remaining white sauce.

6 Preheat the grill to medium-high. Sprinkle the top of the dish
with the Parmesan and place it under the grill for 5–6 minutes
until golden and bubbling. Serve immediately.

Ⓥ **Variation... For a more traditional vegetarian version, see
the recipe on page 102.**

Spicy grilled sardines

Serves 4
284 calories per serving
Takes 10 minutes

4 garlic cloves, crushed
½ teaspoon paprika
1 teaspoon ground cumin
1 tablespoon lemon juice
2 teaspoons olive oil
600 g (1 lb 5 oz) fresh
  sardines, cleaned
salt and freshly ground black
  pepper

This is the sort of dish that is popular in coastal villages all around the Mediterranean. Serve with 30 g (1¼ oz) of dried couscous per person, cooked according to the packet instructions, and a salad.

1 Preheat the grill to high.

2 Mix the garlic with the spices, lemon juice, olive oil and seasoning. Brush this mixture all over the sardines to coat thoroughly.

3 Place the sardines on a rack over the grill pan. Grill for approximately 2 minutes on each side until cooked through.

Tip... One of the easiest ways to make this paste is to put the whole garlic cloves, spices, lemon juice and olive oil in a pestle and mortar and pulvarise together.

Variation... This recipe can be made with 5 x 120 g (4½ oz) canned sardines in brine in exactly the same way, although the cooking time can be reduced to a minute on each side as the fish is already cooked and just needs to be warmed through. This could also be done in a frying pan.

Sicilian beans and vegetables

Serves 4
114 calories per serving
Takes 30 minutes
Ⓥ
❄

calorie controlled cooking spray
3 garlic cloves, chopped
1 orange pepper, de-seeded and sliced
2 courgettes, sliced thickly
1 red chilli, de-seeded and chopped
1 teaspoon dried thyme
2 fresh rosemary sprigs
2 x 400 g cans chopped tomatoes
2 teaspoons tomato purée
400 g can butter beans, drained and rinsed
400 g can artichoke hearts, drained and rinsed
salt and freshly ground black pepper

This is a great meal in itself, or serve as a side dish with meat or fish or as part of a tapas style feast.

1 Spray a heavy based non stick saucepan with the cooking spray and fry the garlic, pepper and courgettes for 3 minutes, adding a splash of water if they start to stick. Add the chilli, thyme and rosemary and then pour in the chopped tomatoes.

2 Stir in the tomato purée and bring to the boil. Reduce the heat and simmer for 10 minutes.

3 Add the butter beans and artichoke hearts and continue to simmer for another 10 minutes, stirring occasionally. Season and serve.

Italian roast chicken

Serves 4

353 calories per serving

Takes 5 minutes to prepare,
20–25 minutes to cook

8 x 85 g (3¼ oz) skinless boneless chicken thighs, trimmed of fat
2 teaspoons low fat spread
2 teaspoons mild chilli powder
½ teaspoon dried oregano or basil
½ teaspoon salt
freshly ground black pepper
a lemon, quartered, to serve

This recipe shows you how to give a tasty twist to the traditional roast. Serve with a crisp green salad and a 225 g (8 oz) potato per person, baked in its skin.

1 Arrange the chicken thighs in a shallow ovenproof baking dish. Preheat the oven to Gas Mark 4/180°C/fan oven 160°C.

2 Beat together the low fat spread, chilli powder, herbs and salt. Dab this mixture on top of the chicken thighs.

3 Season the chicken with pepper and then cover the baking dish loosely with foil. Bake for 20–25 minutes, until the chicken is tender and cooked through.

4 Divide the chicken between four serving plates. Pour over any remaining cooking juices and serve each portion with a lemon quarter.

Red wine braised beef

Serves 4

513 calories per serving

Takes 30 minutes to prepare,
1½ hours to cook

✳

2 tablespoons plain flour

450 g (1 lb) lean stewing
steak, cut into cubes

calorie controlled cooking
spray

100 g (3½ oz) cubed pancetta

10 baby onions, peeled

225 g (8 oz) carrots, peeled
and cut into chunks

50 g (1¾ oz) stoned green
olives in brine, drained

1 bay leaf

1 fresh rosemary sprig

150 ml (5 fl oz) red wine

450 ml (16 fl oz) hot beef
stock

salt and freshly ground black
pepper

To serve

150 g (5½ oz) dried polenta

700 ml (1¼ pts) hot chicken
stock

1 tablespoon fresh thyme
leaves

*This is a rich beef stew, often made with the famous Italian
Barolo wine, and is a great make ahead dinner.*

1 Preheat the oven to Gas Mark 4/180°C/fan oven 160°C.
Place the flour in a shallow dish, season and add the beef,
making sure each piece is coated in the flour.

2 Spray a large, lidded, flameproof and ovenproof casserole
dish with the cooking spray and heat until hot. Add the beef in
batches, cooking and turning until brown. Remove each batch
to a plate before continuing.

3 Spray the casserole dish again and add the pancetta and
onions. Cook for 3–4 minutes and then return the beef to the
dish with the carrots, olives, herbs, wine and stock. Stir well,
bring to the boil and cover. Place in the oven and leave to cook
for 1½ hours until the beef is tender.

4 To make the polenta, place in a pan with the stock and thyme.
Bring to the boil, stirring continuously until thick.

5 Serve the beef with the runny polenta.

Sicilian caponata

Serves 2
207 calories per serving
Takes 10 minutes to prepare,
  20 minutes to cook
Ⓥ

1 red onion, sliced thickly

1 large garlic clove, crushed

1 small aubergine, cut into small cubes

1 courgette, cut into small cubes

1 red pepper, de-seeded and sliced

1 tablespoon olive oil

400 g can chopped tomatoes

1 tablespoon balsamic or red wine vinegar

1 tablespoon lemon juice

2 teaspoons sugar

1 tablespoon capers, drained and rinsed

salt and freshly ground black pepper

Like a sweet and sour ratatouille, this dish can be served hot or cold with 40 g (1½ oz) of dried spaghetti or rice, cooked according to the packet instructions.

1 Place the onion, garlic, aubergine, courgette, pepper, oil and 150 ml (5 fl oz) of water in a large, lidded, non stick saucepan. Heat the mixture until it all starts to sizzle, cover and cook on a medium heat for 10 minutes, stirring once or twice.

2 When the vegetables are softened, add the tomatoes, vinegar, lemon juice, sugar and capers. Season and bring to the boil. Reduce the heat and simmer, uncovered, for about 7–8 minutes. Check the seasoning before serving.

Italian fish stew

Serves 4

183 calories per serving

Takes 30 minutes to prepare,
20 minutes to cook

**calorie controlled cooking
spray**
1 onion, chopped finely
4 garlic cloves, chopped
2 celery sticks, chopped finely
2 carrots, peeled and chopped
400 g can chopped tomatoes
**a small bunch of fresh thyme,
chopped**
1 bay leaf
**grated zest and juice of an
orange**
700 ml (1¼ pints) fish stock
**250 g (9 oz) cod or haddock
fillet, defrosted if frozen and
cut into large cubes**
**250 g (9 oz) mixed seafood,
defrosted if frozen**

To garnish

**a small bunch of fresh parsley,
chopped (optional)**
**2 red chillies, de-seeded and
chopped finely (optional)**

*A colourful fish stew, which you'll find versions of all over
Italy and the Mediterranean.*

1 Heat a large non stick saucepan and spray with the cooking
spray. Add the onion, garlic, celery and carrots. Cook on a low
heat for 10 minutes or until all the vegetables are softened.

2 Add the tomatoes, thyme, bay leaf, orange zest, orange
juice and stock. Bring to the boil and simmer for 20 minutes,
uncovered.

3 Add the fish to the pan and cook for 3 minutes. Finally, add
the seafood and cook for a further 2 minutes.

4 Serve in individual serving bowls, sprinkled with the parsley
and chillies, if using.

Garlic and rosemary leg of lamb

Serves 4
257 calories per serving
Takes 10 minutes to prepare
 + marinating + 15 minutes
 standing, 1½ hours to cook
❄

1 kg (2 lb 4 oz) leg of lamb
4 garlic cloves, sliced
8 small fresh rosemary sprigs
1 orange, cut into thin slices
1 tablespoon clear honey
salt and freshly ground black
 pepper

A perfect Sunday lunch served with freshly cooked veggies.

1 Rinse the lamb and pat dry. Lift into a shallow non metallic dish.

2 Make random slits all over the top of the lamb and insert the slices of garlic and rosemary sprigs. Arrange the orange slices over the top and season well. Cover and leave to marinate for at least 3 hours or preferably overnight.

3 Preheat the oven to Gas Mark 6/200°C/fan oven 180°C. Lift the lamb into a roasting tin, removing the orange slices, and cook for 1 hour. Brush the top with honey and return to the oven for 30 minutes. Allow to stand for 15 minutes before carving. Serve 3 x 35 g (1¼ oz) slices per person.

Italian baked courgettes

Serves 4

154 calories per serving

Takes 15 minutes to prepare,
  25 minutes to cook

Ⓥ

2 medium slices wholewheat
  bread
700 g (1 lb 9 oz) courgettes
a small bunch of fresh
  marjoram
2 eggs, beaten
4 tablespoons skimmed milk
100 g (3½ oz) low fat natural
  yogurt
100 g (3½ oz) low fat soft
  cheese
salt and freshly ground black
  pepper

This is a wonderful way to add interest to courgettes.

1 Preheat the grill to high. Whizz the bread to crumbs in a food processor.

2 Slice the courgettes diagonally into 1 cm (½ inch) thick long slices and lay them on a large baking tray. Place under the grill for 5 minutes or until blackening at the edges and slightly dried out.

3 Preheat the oven to Gas Mark 5/190°C/fan oven 170°C. Place one third of the courgettes in the bottom of an ovenproof dish and then scatter with one third of the marjoram.

4 Beat together the eggs, milk, yogurt and cheese and season. Pour one third of this mixture over the courgettes and marjoram. Repeat the layers until all the courgettes and marjoram are used up.

5 Sprinkle the top layer with the breadcrumbs and bake for 25 minutes or until the top is golden.

One tray roast chicken

Serves 4
331 calories per serving
Takes 20 minutes to prepare,
30 minutes to cook

**600 g (1 lb 5 oz) baby new
potatoes, halved**

**grated zest and juice of a
lemon**

**2 tablespoons chopped fresh
thyme or rosemary**

2 garlic cloves, crushed

**4 x 165 g (5¾ oz) chicken
quarters, skin removed
(see Tip)**

4 leeks, each cut into 3 chunks

**1 red pepper, de-seeded and
chopped roughly**

**1 yellow pepper, de-seeded
and chopped roughly**

**calorie controlled cooking
spray**

200 g (7 oz) cherry tomatoes

freshly ground black pepper

*An easy mid week roast that will please the whole family
and get them eating their vegetables. With everything
roasted together in one tray, it also saves on washing up.*

1 Preheat the oven to Gas Mark 6/200°C/ fan oven 180°C.
Bring a saucepan of water to the boil, add the potatoes and
cook for 10 minutes, until just tender.

2 Meanwhile, mix the lemon zest with the herbs and garlic.
Lightly slash the chicken quarters using a sharp knife and rub
the herb mixture all over and into the chicken.

3 Drain the potatoes well and tip them into a large roasting
tin. Add the leeks and peppers and spray the vegetables with
the cooking spray. Arrange the chicken joints on top, drizzle the
lemon juice over and season lightly with black pepper.

4 Roast for 10 minutes, stir everything around and then return
the tin to the oven for a further 10 minutes. Add the cherry
tomatoes, stir again so that everything browns evenly and then
roast for a final 10 minutes. Check that the chicken is cooked
through by piercing the thickest part of the joints with a sharp
knife – the juices should run clear.

Tip... It's much easier to skin chicken joints if you grasp
the skin with kitchen towel. This gives you a better grip,
enabling you to easily pull the skin away from the flesh.

Sole Florentine

Serves 2

286 calories per serving

Takes 15 minutes to prepare,
30–35 minutes to cook

✲

250 g (9 oz) spinach, washed

calorie controlled cooking
spray

2 tomatoes, skinned and
sliced

250 g (9 oz) lemon sole fillets

a few drops of lemon juice

60 g (2 oz) low fat soft cheese

3 tablespoons very low fat
plain fromage frais

15 g (½ oz) half fat mature
Cheddar cheese, grated
finely

1 tablespoon fresh white
breadcrumbs

1 tablespoon finely grated
Parmesan cheese

salt and freshly ground black
pepper

fresh parsley sprigs, to
garnish

This Mediterranean recipe for sole fillets cooked with spinach, tomatoes and soft cheese sauce is so easy and quick to make. Delicious served alone, or with plenty of vegetables.

1 Preheat the oven to Gas Mark 5/190°C/fan oven 170°C.

2 Pack the spinach into a large saucepan and cook, without adding any water, for 3–4 minutes until the leaves have wilted. Drain well, squeezing out any excess moisture with the back of a spoon. Cool and chop roughly.

3 Lightly spray a 1 litre (1¾ pint) ovenproof baking dish with the cooking spray. Spread the spinach over the base and top with the sliced tomatoes. Season and then lay the sole fillets on top. Season once more and sprinkle over the lemon juice.

4 Place the soft cheese, fromage frais and Cheddar cheese in a small saucepan and heat gently, stirring until combined. Spread this sauce evenly over the fish.

5 Sprinkle the surface with the breadcrumbs and Parmesan cheese and then transfer to the oven. Bake for 30–35 minutes. Serve garnished with the parsley.

Tip... For a hint of garlic, choose low fat soft cheese flavoured with garlic and herbs.

Variation... Try making this dish with coley instead of lemon sole.

Couscous stuffed red peppers

Serves 2

174 calories per serving

Takes 15 minutes to prepare,
15–20 minutes to cook

**calorie controlled cooking
spray**

**2 large red peppers, halved
and de-seeded**

50 g (1¾ oz) dried couscous

½ a kettleful of boiling water

**5 cm (2 inches) cucumber,
finely chopped**

2 tomatoes, finely chopped

**1 tablespoon chopped fresh
coriander**

**salt and freshly ground black
pepper**

*This is a vegetarian alternative of the Lamb stuffed red
peppers on page 140.*

1 Preheat the oven to Gas Mark 4/180°C/fan oven 160°C.
Spray an ovenproof dish with the cooking spray and place the
peppers in the dish.

2 Place the couscous in a bowl, pour over boiling water to
cover, cover with cling film and leave to soak for 10 minutes.

3 Fluff up the couscous with a fork and mix in the cucumber,
tomatoes and coriander. Season.

4 Spoon the couscous mixture into the red peppers. Bake for
15–20 minutes. Serve immediately.

Tip... Always wash your hands and the knife you have been
using after chopping chillies, and be careful not to touch
your eyes until you have done this – it will burn.

Chicken with porcini pesto

Serves 1
420 calories per serving
Takes 35 minutes

**15 g (½ oz) dried porcini
mushrooms**
15 g (½ oz) pine nut kernels
**1 tablespoon low fat soft
cheese with garlic and herbs**
**150 g (5½ oz) skinless
boneless chicken breast**

For the sauce
**calorie controlled cooking
spray**
1 shallot, sliced
**100 g (3½ oz) mushrooms,
sliced**
**½ teaspoon dried oregano or
marjoram**
1 tablespoon dry white wine
**1 tablespoon half fat crème
fraîche**
**salt and freshly ground black
pepper**

*Serve with lots of green beans or a mixed salad, drizzled
with balsamic vinegar.*

1 Put the porcini mushrooms in a small bowl and cover with
hot water. Leave to soak for 5 minutes and then drain and
chop.

2 Meanwhile, dry fry the pine nut kernels in a small non stick
frying pan until they are golden brown. Be careful not to let
them burn. Preheat the grill to high.

3 Mix the porcini mushrooms with the pine nut kernels and
soft cheese. Slit the chicken breast on the side to make a
pocket and fill the pocket with the cheese mixture.

4 Grill the chicken breast for 4–5 minutes on each side,
spooning any filling that comes out on to the top.

5 Meanwhile, heat a non stick frying pan and spray with the
cooking spray. Fry the shallot until softened.

6 With the heat high, add the mushrooms and herbs, season
and stir fry for 1 minute. Add the wine and bubble for a few
seconds, incorporating any browned juices from the pan with
a wooden spoon.

7 Turn down the heat and add the crème fraîche. Stir until
hot, but do not allow to boil. Spoon the sauce over the chicken
to serve.

Mediterranean turkey rolls

Serves 4

217 calories per serving

Takes 45 minutes + cooling

2 aubergines

2 red peppers

100 g (3½ oz) ricotta

a large bunch of fresh basil, chopped, with a few chopped leaves reserved

8 x 50 g (1¾ oz) thin turkey escalopes

calorie controlled cooking spray

1 garlic clove, crushed

2 tablespoons white wine vinegar

400 g can chopped tomatoes

1 teaspoon clear honey

salt and freshly ground black pepper

Basil complements turkey so well in these tasty rolls that the whole family will love.

1 Preheat the oven to Gas Mark 6/200°C/fan oven 180°C. Place the whole aubergines and red peppers on a baking tray and bake for 20 minutes. Set aside to cool.

2 Meanwhile, put the ricotta in a bowl with half the basil and season. Season the turkey escalopes and then put them between two sheets of baking parchment, foil or cling film. Beat with a rolling pin or meat tenderising mallet until thin but not broken.

3 When the peppers are cool enough to handle, peel and de-seed them and then chop them finely. Mix with the ricotta and remaining basil. Put spoonfuls of this along one end of the turkey escalopes and then roll them up.

4 Line a baking tray with foil and spray with the cooking spray. Place the rolls on the foil and bake in the oven for 10 minutes until golden and cooked through.

5 Meanwhile, slice the aubergines in half lengthwise, scoop out all the flesh and chop well. Spray a non stick frying pan with the cooking spray, sauté the garlic for 2 minutes and then add the white wine vinegar and aubergine flesh.

6 Cook for 2 minutes, stirring, and then add the tomatoes, reserved basil leaves and honey. Season and cook for 10 minutes. Check the seasoning and then serve poured over the turkey rolls.

Lamb stuffed red peppers

Serves 2

317 calories per serving

Takes 10 minutes to prepare,
35–45 minutes to cook

calorie controlled cooking
spray

2 large red peppers, halved
and de-seeded

1 small onion, chopped

1 teaspoon chopped fresh root
ginger

1 garlic clove, crushed

½ teaspoon garam masala

200 g (7 oz) lamb mince

½ green chilli, de-seeded and
chopped finely

1 tablespoon chopped fresh
coriander

salt and freshly ground black
pepper

*Serve with a green vegetable such as broccoli and
100 g (3½ oz) of new potatoes per person.*

1 Preheat the oven to Gas Mark 4/180°C/fan oven 160°C.
Spray an ovenproof dish with the cooking spray and place the
peppers in the dish.

2 Spray a non stick frying pan with the cooking spray and fry
the onion until golden.

3 Lower the heat and add the ginger, garlic and garam masala.
Season and stir fry for 2–3 minutes.

4 Add the lamb and fry for about 10–12 minutes. Add the
chilli and coriander and stir fry for another 2–3 minutes.

5 Spoon the lamb mixture into the red peppers. Bake for
15–20 minutes. Serve immediately.

Variations... Other coloured peppers or large beefsteak
tomatoes could also be used in this recipe – make the
filling in the same way and stuff the vegetables before
placing in the oven. Tomatoes will take slightly less time
to cook.

ⓥ For a fantastic vegetarian version, see the recipe on
page 136.

Mackerel with Parma ham

Serves 2

475 calories per serving

Takes 25 minutes to prepare,
  15 minutes to cook

**350 g (12 oz) potatoes,
  chopped**

**1 tablespoon horseradish
  sauce**

**4 slices Parma ham, cut in half
  lengthways**

**4 x 60 g (2 oz) mackerel fillets,
  cut in half lengthways**

*The horseradish mash adds a touch of warmth to this very
flavourful dish. Serve with steamed broccoli.*

1 Bring a large saucepan of water to the boil, add the
potatoes and cook for 15 minutes until tender. Drain, reserving
2 tablespoons of the cooking liquid.

2 Mash the potatoes with the reserved cooking liquid and
the horseradish. Keep warm.

3 Preheat the grill to medium. Wrap a strip of Parma ham
around each mackerel fillet and grill, skin side up, for
8–10 minutes, turning occasionally, until browned and
cooked through.

4 Serve the mackerel wrapped in Parma ham with the mash
on the side.

One pot Italian beef stew

Serves 4

356 calories per serving

Takes 25 minutes to prepare,
1 hour 50 minutes to cook

❋ (before adding the pasta)

calorie controlled cooking
spray

600 g (1 lb 5 oz) lean beef
stewing steak, diced

1 large onion, sliced

6 garlic cloves, peeled

1 tablespoon fresh chopped
rosemary

12 stoned black olives in
brine, drained

400 g can chopped tomatoes

1 litre (1¾ pints) beef stock

125 g (4½ oz) dried wholemeal
pasta shapes, e.g. fusilli

freshly ground black pepper

This is a great all-in-one filling family casserole, containing meat, vegetables and pasta.

1 Preheat the oven to Gas Mark 1/140°C/ fan oven 120°C. Heat a non stick frying pan, spray with the cooking spray and brown the beef in two batches, transferring the meat to a plate as it is done.

2 At the same time, heat a large, lidded, flameproof and ovenproof casserole dish, spray with the cooking spray and brown the onion, adding a splash of water if it starts to stick.

3 Add the whole garlic cloves, rosemary, olives and chopped tomatoes to the casserole dish. Pour a little of the stock into the frying pan and stir to release the meat browning juices. Add this to the casserole, along with the rest of the stock. Add the beef to the casserole and bring it to a simmer. Cover and transfer to the oven to cook for 1½ hours.

4 Stir the pasta into the casserole, pushing it down into the liquid. Replace the lid and return the casserole to the oven to cook for 15–20 minutes, until the pasta is tender. Season and serve immediately.

Italian chicken meatballs

Serves 4

230 calories per serving

Takes 30 minutes to prepare,
40 minutes to cook

❄

1 teaspoon olive oil

1 red onion, chopped very
finely

1 garlic clove, crushed

1 teaspoon dried oregano

450 g (1 lb) chicken mince

50 g (1¾ oz) fresh white
breadcrumbs

1 egg

400 g can chopped tomatoes

300 ml (10 fl oz) chicken stock

2 tablespoons tomato purée

3 tablespoons dry white wine

100 g (3½ oz) button
mushrooms, sliced

salt and freshly ground black
pepper

Meatballs made with chicken instead of beef make a healthier dish, but are just as tasty.

1 Heat the olive oil in a small, lidded, non stick saucepan and add the onion and garlic with 1 tablespoon of water. Cover and cook over a low heat for 5 minutes, until the onion has softened.

2 Place the oregano, chicken, breadcrumbs and egg in a mixing bowl with the garlic and onion. Season, mix together thoroughly and then, using wet hands, roll the mixture into 20 small balls.

3 Place the remaining ingredients in a medium lidded saucepan. Stir well and bring to the boil. Add the chicken meatballs, season and reduce the heat. Cover and simmer for 40 minutes, stirring from time to time.

Tip... The poached chicken meatballs will have quite a soft texture. For a firmer texture, cook the sauce separately for 15 minutes and arrange the meatballs on a baking tray lined with non stick baking parchment. Spray with calorie controlled cooking spray and bake at Gas Mark 5/190°C/fan oven 170°C for 20 minutes. Heat them in the sauce for 5 minutes.

Ⓥ **Variation...** For a vegetarian version, substitute Quorn mince for the chicken.

Desserts and bakes

Orange panna cotta

Serves 6

106 calories per serving

Takes 20 minutes to prepare
 + 45 minutes standing,
 2–3 hours to chill

4 gelatine leaves

1 large orange

300 ml (10 fl oz) skimmed milk

**1 tablespoon artificial
sweetener**

**2 tablespoons orange flower
water (optional)**

**150 g (5½ oz) low fat soft
cheese**

**2 x 125 g pots low fat Greek
style orange yogurt**

15–20 ice cubes

*This stunning dessert is smooth and creamy with a real
citrus kick. Chill in the fridge for up to 3 days.*

1 Line a 21 x 8 cm (8½ x 3¼ inch), 1.2 litre (2 pint) loaf tin
with cling film (it helps to first brush the tin with a little cold
water) and put it into the fridge. Put the gelatine leaves into
a small bowl and cover with cold water. Set aside.

2 Grate the orange zest finely and put it in a small saucepan.
Add the milk and sweetener and bring to a simmer. Remove
from the heat. Squeeze the water out of the gelatine leaves and
stir the leaves into the warm milk until smooth and melted.

3 Put the orange flower water (if using), soft cheese and
yogurt into a jug. Gradually pour the warm milk mixture into
the yogurt, beating after each addition until smooth. Put the
ice into a large bowl and top up with a little cold water. Stand
the jug in the middle of the iced water (this will help chill the
mixture) and set aside for 45 minutes, stirring occasionally
until the mixture is the thickness of whipped double cream.

4 Meanwhile, cut the top and base off the orange and stand
upright on a board. Using a serrated knife, carefully cut away
the peel and pith and then cut the orange into thin slices.
Remove the loaf tin from the fridge and arrange the orange
slices in a row along the base.

5 Pour the thickened milk mixture over the oranges and chill
in the fridge for 2–3 hours until set. To serve, turn out on to a
serving platter, remove the cling film and cut into six slices.

Lemon granita

Serves 4
100 calories per serving
Takes 10 minutes to prepare
  + freezing
🅥
❄

finely grated zest of 2 lemons,
  plus the juice of 3
6 tablespoons caster sugar

Granita is great as a palate cleanser or a refreshing dessert.

1 Place the lemon zest and juice and sugar in a pan and bring to the boil. Simmer for 5–6 minutes until syrupy. Pour the syrup into a measuring jug and make up to 600 ml (20 fl oz) with cold water.

2 Pour into a shallow metal tray and freeze for about an hour.

3 Every hour, remove the tray from the freezer and scrape the ice to break it up into slushy crystals. Do this for about 4 hours. Store in a freezerproof lidded plastic box until required.

Variation... For a coffee version, see the recipe on page 158.

Tiramisu pots

Serves 4
121 calories per serving
Takes 10 minutes

8 Savoiardi biscuits or sponge fingers
1 cup strong cold black coffee
350 g (12 oz) low fat vanilla yogurt
100 g (3½ oz) Quark
15 g (½ oz) plain chocolate, grated

This moreish dessert is literally whipped up in a matter of minutes.

1 Dip two of the biscuits or fingers in the cold coffee, making sure they do not go too soggy. Cut each in half and place all the pieces in the bottom of a ramekin or glass. Repeat with the remaining six biscuits and a further three ramekins.

2 Whisk together the yogurt and Quark and spoon a quarter of it into each ramekin. Sprinkle the tops with the chocolate.

Variation... Try adding a layer of your favourite fruit on top of the coffee-soaked biscuits. Use ½ sliced small banana per pot.

Zuccotto

Serves 4

155 calories per serving

Takes 30 minutes to prepare
+ 2–3 hours chilling,
15 minutes to cook

Ⓥ

40 g (1½ oz) self raising flour
15 g (½ oz) cornflour
2 teaspoons cocoa powder
2 eggs, separated
40 g (1½ oz) icing sugar
1 teaspoon rum essence

For the filling

**100 g (3½ oz) fresh cherries,
stoned**
**100 g (3½ oz) very low fat
plain fromage frais**
**2 teaspoons artificial
sweetener**

This Italian dessert is sure to impress any guests.

1 Preheat the oven to Gas Mark 4/180°C/fan oven 160°C and line a 20 cm (8 inch) round cake tin with non stick baking parchment.

2 Sift the flour, cornflour and cocoa powder together in a large bowl. Beat the egg yolks until pale and thick and then whisk in half the icing sugar. Add the yolk mixture to the flour but do not mix it in yet.

3 In a clean, grease-free bowl, whisk the egg whites until they form stiff peaks. Whisk in the other half of the icing sugar, reserving 1 teaspoon for dusting.

4 Very gently fold both the yolk mixture and the egg white mixture into the flour with the rum essence. Spoon into the prepared tin and bake in the oven for 15 minutes. Remove from the tin and cool on a wire rack. The sponge will be quite thin.

5 Meanwhile, place the cherries and a little water in a pan, bring to a simmer, cook until soft and then leave to cool. In a bowl, mix the cherries with the fromage frais and sweetener.

6 When the sponge is cool, slice it in half to make two rounds. Use one to line a 600 ml (20 fl oz) pudding basin, cutting it to fit the bottom and the sides. Spoon in the cherry mixture and then use the other sponge half as the lid, cutting it to fit.

7 Press down on the sponge lid and place a saucer on top. Place a weight like a can of beans on top of the saucer. Chill for a few hours and then turn out on to a serving plate. Sprinkle with the reserved icing sugar and serve.

Coffee granita

Serves 4

17 calories per serving

Takes 10 minutes to prepare
+ freezing

Ⓥ

❄

2 tablespoons instant coffee
1 tablespoon caster sugar
¼ kettleful of boiling water

Lighter than ice cream, a granita is a semi-frozen dessert similar to sorbet.

1 Place the coffee and sugar in a measuring jug and add a little boiling water, just enough to dissolve both. Make up to 600 ml (20 fl oz) with cold water.

2 Pour into a shallow metal tray and freeze for about an hour.

3 Every hour, remove the tray from the freezer and scrape the ice to break it up into slushy crystals for about 4 hours. Store in a freezerproof, lidded plastic box until required.

Variation... For a zingy lemon version, see the recipe on page 152.

Zabaglione

Serves 4
150 calories per serving
Takes 25 minutes + chilling

1 sachet lemon pie filling
1 egg, separated
25 g (1 oz) caster sugar
100 ml (3½ fl oz) white wine
100 g (3½ oz) low fat plain
   fromage frais
a few drops of lemon juice
artificial sweetener, to taste
   (optional)
1 square of chocolate, grated

This healthier option Italian inspired dessert is absolutely scrumptious.

1 Empty the sachet of lemon pie filling into a saucepan and blend in 250 ml (9 fl oz) of cold water and the egg yolk. Cook gently, stirring constantly, until the mixture boils and thickens, checking that the flavour capsule dissolves if there is one. Remove from the heat and allow to cool for a few minutes.

2 In a clean, grease-free bowl, whisk the egg white until it forms stiff peaks and then whisk in the caster sugar. Add the wine and the slightly cooled lemon mixture, folding in gently to combine.

3 Divide the mixture between four serving glasses, cool completely and then cover and chill in the fridge.

4 Just before serving, flavour the fromage frais with a little lemon juice and artificial sweetener (if desired) and use to top the desserts. Finish off with the grated chocolate.

Tip... Remember that egg white will not whisk successfully if there is the slightest trace of grease or egg yolk in the bowl or on the beaters. It's always a good precaution to wash the bowl and beaters in hot soapy water before you begin.

Italian trifle

Serves 4

284 calories per serving

Takes 5 minutes to prepare +
30 minutes chilling

Ⓨ

4 trifle sponges
250 g (9 oz) ricotta
**100 g (3½ oz) low fat soft
cheese**
**2 tablespoons reduced sugar
jam with extra fruit**
**450 g (1 lb) mixed
strawberries, raspberries
and blueberries, defrosted
if frozen**
**400 g can peach slices in
natural juice**
2 drops vanilla essence
fresh mint leaves, to decorate

This velvety smooth Italian dessert is absolutely delicious.

1 Line the bottom of a large glass trifle bowl or four individual bowls with the trifle sponges.

2 In a separate bowl, beat together the ricotta, soft cheese and jam.

3 Quarter the strawberries, if using fresh ones. Reserving a few berries for decoration, mix with the other berries, peach slices and juice and vanilla essence in a bowl. Spoon this mixture over the sponges.

4 Spread the cheese mixture evenly over the fruit and decorate with the reserved berries and the mint leaves. Refrigerate for at least 30 minutes before serving.

Almond meringue peaches

Serves 4
133 calories per recipe
Takes 20 minutes
Ⓥ

**4 ripe peaches, stoned and
halved**
8 amaretti biscuits
**2 tablespoons Amaretto or
Cointreau liqueur**
1 egg white
30 g (1¼ oz) caster sugar
15 g (½ oz) flaked almonds

*Make these in the summer when peaches are at their
sweetest juiciest best.*

1 Preheat the grill to medium. Place the peach halves, hollow
side up, in a tart or Yorkshire pudding baking tin that will fit in
your grill pan (the holes in the tin will help keep the peaches
upright).

2 Place a biscuit in each peach hollow and drizzle a little of the
liqueur over each.

3 In a clean, grease-free bowl, whisk the egg white until stiff
peaks form and then gradually whisk in the caster sugar. Put a
spoonful of meringue over each peach.

4 Place under the grill and cook slowly for 3–4 minutes. Watch
to make sure they don't start to brown too quickly. Sprinkle the
almonds over the top and continue to grill until the meringue
and nuts have turned golden. Transfer the peaches to four
small plates and serve immediately.

Chocolate chestnut cake

Makes 10 slices

170 calories per serving

Takes 20 minutes to prepare
+ 30 minutes chilling +
cooling, 20 minutes to bake

Ⓥ

This is the lightest chocolate sponge filled with a creamy chocolate and chestnut cream that's thoroughly indulgent.

1 Preheat the oven to Gas Mark 4/180°C/fan oven 160°C. Spray two 18 cm (7 inch) non stick cake tins with the cooking spray.

2 Cream the low fat spread and sugar together until fluffy, either in a food processor or by hand, and then add the eggs one at a time, beating well between each addition. Sift in the flour and cocoa powder and mix thoroughly.

3 Spoon equal amounts of the cake mixture into each prepared tin and bake for 20 minutes until risen and a skewer, when inserted in the middle, comes out clean.

4 Turn out the cakes on to wire racks to cool.

calorie controlled cooking
   spray
100 g (3½ oz) low fat spread
100 g (3½ oz) caster sugar
2 eggs
100 g (3½ oz) self raising flour
25 g (1 oz) unsweetened
   cocoa powder
icing sugar, for dusting

For the filling

200 g (7 oz) unsweetened
   chestnut purée
50 g (1¾ oz) plain chocolate
   (minimum 70% cocoa
   solids), melted
200 g (7 oz) low fat soft
   cheese
1 teaspoon vanilla essence

5 When cool, slice each cake in half horizontally to make four discs. Mix all the filling ingredients together. Place one cake disc on a plate and spread it with a quarter of the filling. Top with another disc and repeat until all four discs are used. Decorate with mounds of the remaining filling. Refrigerate for 30 minutes before serving and then dust with icing sugar.

Tip... Chestnut pureé can be found in most supermarkets, usually in the gravy and stuffings section.

Caraway grissini

Makes 12

30 calories per serving

Takes 25 minutes to prepare + 30–40 minutes rising + cooling, 15–20 minutes to bake

Ⓥ

❄

calorie controlled cooking spray

1 garlic clove, chopped finely

100 g (3½ oz) strong white bread flour, 2 teaspoons reserved for rolling

½ teaspoon salt

1 teaspoon caraway seeds

½ teaspoon easy blend yeast

sea salt flakes

These rustic breadsticks are very useful for a lunch box or a great way to enjoy dips.

1 Lightly coat a small non stick frying pan with the cooking spray and heat until hot. Add the garlic and cook for 2–3 minutes until beginning to brown.

2 Put the flour and salt in a bowl and stir in the garlic and caraway seeds. Blend the yeast with 75 ml (3 fl oz) of warm water and pour over the flour. Mix to a soft dough, kneading lightly, and then cover and leave in a warm place to double in size for 20–30 minutes.

3 Preheat the oven to Gas Mark 6/200°C/fan oven 180°C. Line a baking tray with non stick baking parchment.

4 Dust the work surface with the reserved flour and form the dough into a ball, kneading lightly. Divide into 12 equal pieces. Roll each into a thin sausage about 20 cm (8 inches) long and place on the baking tray. Leave for 10 minutes to rise a little, spray with the cooking spray, sprinkle with sea salt flakes and bake for 15–20 minutes until golden and crisp.

Tip... Store the breadsticks in an airtight container for up to 4 days.

Fennel biscuits

Makes 16

89 calories per serving

Takes 10 minutes to prepare +
  cooling, 15 minutes to bake

Ⓥ

75 ml (3 fl oz) olive oil

75 ml (3 fl oz) medium white
  wine

50 g (1¾ oz) golden caster
  sugar

125 g (4½ oz) plain flour

½ teaspoon baking powder

1 teaspoon finely grated
  lemon zest

1 teaspoon fennel seeds

2 teaspoons icing sugar, for
  dusting

*These aniseed flavoured biscuits have a slightly crunchy
outer layer with a spongy inner one, similar to soft
amaretti.*

1 Preheat the oven to Gas Mark 4/180°C/fan oven 160°C.
Line two baking trays with non stick baking parchment.

2 Place the oil, wine and sugar in a bowl. Beat vigorously to
combine.

3 Sift the flour and baking powder together and fold into the
sugar mixture with the lemon zest and fennel seeds. Place
teaspoonfuls on the trays, spaced well apart as they will
spread. Bake for 15 minutes until set (they will change a little
in colour).

4 Remove from the oven and cool on the trays for 5 minutes
before transferring to a wire rack to cool completely. Dust with
the icing sugar. Store in an airtight container for up to 3 days.

Variation... You could try a teaspoon of orange zest with
½ a teaspoon of cinnamon in place of the lemon and
fennel.

Lemon polenta cake

Serves 12

158 calories per serving

Takes 15 minutes to prepare + cooling, 30 minutes to bake

Ⓥ

calorie controlled cooking spray

115 g (4 oz) dried polenta (ordinary or quick cook)

115 g (4 oz) plain flour

1½ teaspoons baking powder

2 large eggs, plus 3 egg whites

175 g (6 oz) caster sugar

grated zest and juice of 2 lemons

1 teaspoon vanilla extract

200 ml (7 fl oz) low fat natural yogurt

icing sugar, for dusting

Polenta colours this cake a pretty yellow and gives it a subtle crunch. Serve warm or cold, cut into slices, with fresh strawberries and 1 tablespoon of half fat crème fraîche per person.

1 Preheat the oven to Gas Mark 4/180°C/fan oven 160°C. Spray the base of a 25 cm (10 inch) springform cake tin with the cooking spray. Dust the tin with a little polenta.

2 Sift the flour and baking powder together into a bowl and then stir in the polenta.

3 In a separate bowl, whisk the whole eggs, egg whites and sugar together until pale and thick.

4 Add the polenta mixture, lemon zest and juice, vanilla extract and yogurt. Carefully fold in using a large metal spoon.

5 Spoon the mixture into the prepared tin and bake for 30 minutes.

6 Turn out on to a cooling rack and dust with icing sugar to serve.

Focaccia bread

Serves 4

247 calories per serving

Takes 20 minutes to prepare
+ 30 minutes rising,
10–15 minutes to bake

Ⓥ

2 teaspoons dried yeast

1 teaspoon caster sugar

calorie controlled cooking
spray

2 x 145 g packets pizza dough
mix

1 teaspoon plain flour, for
flouring

1 teaspoon olive oil, for
greasing

2–3 fresh rosemary sprigs,
leaves only

sea salt

This soft bread can be served with salad and cheese or as a sweet topped with fruit, yogurt and honey.

1 In a small mixing bowl, combine the yeast, sugar and 225 ml (8 fl oz) of warm water and leave for 15 minutes until frothy. Spray a 28 x 18 cm (11 x 7 inch) shallow baking tin with the cooking spray.

2 Put the pizza mix into a large bowl and make a well in the centre. Add the frothed yeast and mix to a soft dough. Turn out on to a floured surface and knead for 2–3 minutes until smooth in texture.

3 Press into the prepared baking tin, pushing the dough into the corners. Cover with cling film, oiled with the olive oil, and leave to rise in a warm place for about 30 minutes or until doubled in height.

4 Meanwhile, preheat the oven to Gas Mark 7/220°C/fan oven 200°C. Make dimples all over the surface of the risen dough with your fingers and sprinkle with the rosemary and sea salt.

5 Bake for 10–15 minutes until golden.

Variation... To make a sweet version, add 1 tablespoon of caster sugar to the dry pizza mix before adding the yeast. Sprinkle a little demerara sugar over the finished dough in the tray instead of the rosemary and salt.

Index